Three cities dominate Western culture since Antiquity: Jerusalem, the origin of faith; Athens, the academe of reason; and Alexandria, the cradle of gnosis and imagination. This last perennial stream of tradition remained virtually unknown until the discovery of gnostic manuscripts in Egypt in 1945.

June Singer is the most profound and thoughtful of psychologists I know, and she was schooled in the workshops of William Blake. Therefore she is best equipped to introduce as Anglo-Saxon reader into this unexplored field of knowledge of the heart.

Professor Gilles Quispel
Ancient Professor of Religion at Utrecht and Harvard Universities

In Knowledge of the Heart, June Singer rescues ancient Gnostic scriptures from obscurity and makes this relevant to our daily lives. It is rare to find a book that successfully blends mysticism and psychology in this fashion. *Knowledge of the Heart* deserves a wide audience.

Jay Kinney
Editor-in-chief, *Gnosis* Magazine

In Knowledge of the Heart, June Singer, the distinguished Jungian analyst, turns metaphysical tales into psychological ones. The journey of the Gnostic soul from the godhead to the material world and back becomes a symbol of the journey of the psyche from unconsciousness to consciousness and reconnection to consciousness.

In the style for which she is so admired and loved, Singer in turn translates Jungian lingo into heartfelt, everyday language. The Gnostic search for wholeness becomes a model for the universal quest for harmony in all of one's life. No special commitment to Jungian principles is needed to appreciate that message.

Professor Robert A. Segal
Professor of Religious Studies at the University of Lancaster,
and Editor of *The Gnostic Jung*

This book, written by a Jungian analyst who has had a lifetime of experience with matters of the heart and gnosticism, presents an easily accessible and readable introduction to the subject of gnosticism. In the introduction she presents a lucid account of the many elements which make up gnosticism. She makes an important distinction between Gnosticism, a major religion in the early Christian era, and gnosticism as the experience of inner revealed truth. She uses writings from the early Gnostics to speak about gnosticism as inner truth.

In the body of the book she presents selections of new translations from the *Nag Hammadi*, and *The Gnostic Scriptures* by Bentley Leyton. These texts have great psychological relevance, and their mythological qualities are used to demonstrate the "awesome mysteries." With each set of meditations she offers interpretations which apply to the meditation and which give each a deeper sense of meaning. As I read the book, I let myself feel into the individual meditation and go with it. The experience of reading this book is bound to open the heart.

THOMAS B. KIRSCH, M.D.,
Past-President of the International Association of Analytical Psychologists,
and author of *The History of Jungian Psychology*

Fascinating, unique, and glowing with the mystery of gnosis, Dr. Singer's book captures the timeless essence of these ancient texts. With clarity and beauty, this presentation achieves a profound revelation of Gnostic material and of the human soul. This perceptively sensitive work is destined to become a classic.

BISHOP ROSAMONDE MILLER,
Presiding Bishop, The Church of Gnosis

June Singer PhD is a Jungian Analyst, and she lectures and conducts workshops around the world. She is the author of a number of books including the bestselling *Boundaries of the Soul*.

by the same author

Androgyny: The Opposites Within

Boundaries of the Soul: The Practice of Jung's Psychology

Modern Woman in Search of Soul

The Unholy Bible: Blake, Jung and the Collective Unconscious

KNOWLEDGE OF THE HEART

GNOSTIC SECRETS OF INNER WISDOM

JUNE SINGER

Shaftesbury, Dorset • Boston, Massachusetts • Melbourne, Victoria

Revised edition © Element Books Limited 1999
Text © June Singer 1999

Originally published in 1992 as
A Gnostic Book of Hours

This edition first published in the UK in 1999 by
Element Books Limited
Shaftesbury, Dorset SP7 8BP

Published in the USA in 1999 by
Element Books, Inc.
160 North Washington Street
Boston, MA 02114

Published in Australia in 1999 by
Element Books and distributed
by Penguin Australia Limited
487 Maroondah Highway, Ringwood,
Victoria 3134

June Singer has asserted her right under the
Copyright, Designs and Patents Act, 1988, to be
identified as author of this work.

Designed and typeset by Mark Slader
Printed and bound in the USA

British Library Cataloguing in Publication data available

Library of Congress Cataloging in Publication data available

ISBN 1 86204 539 9

Selections from the *Nag Hammadi Library* in English, revised edition by James M.
Robinson, © E.J. Brill, Leiden, The Netherlands, 1988; reprinted by permission of
HarperCollins Publishers., New York, and Taylor and Francis, London.

CONTENTS

EARLY MORNING MEDITATIONS

MID-MORNING MEDITATIONS

MIDDAY MEDITATIONS

AFTERNOON MEDITATIONS

MEDITATIONS AT SUNSET

NIGHT MEDITATIONS

For

Professor Gilles Quispel,
editor of *The Jung Codex*

whose scholarship and inner wisdom
provided the thread that led me through
the labyrinthine ways of gnosis.

Acknowledgements

M Y FIRST DEBT IS TO BISHOP Rosamonde Miller of the
Gnostic Center in Palo Alto, California, who has shown
me how gnostic ideas can be expressed in a beautiful contemporary ritual that is satisfying both spiritually and psychologically.
I acknowledge also my late friend, the Reverend Father Alcuin
Anastasios, a monk and an abbot, who knew more about Books
of Hours and spiritual practice and the history of the Early
Church than I can ever hope to know. He read my manuscript in
its various stages, made comments and suggestions, and let me
know when I overstated, understated or just plain misstated,
and all through this his encouragement supported me. Professor
Gilles Quispel recognized my very early interest in Gnosticism
when I was doing research for my book *Androgyny* more than a
decade ago, and he has been consistently affirming of my
efforts. Professor Elaine Pagels provided further stimulus for
my exploration of modern gnosticism when she agreed to share a
seminar platform with me on the subject, "Little known stories
about Adam and Eve," for the Association for Transpersonal
Psychology. Jungian analyst, Aryeh Maidenbaum provided the
impetus that made this edition of the book possible. Ian Fenton
envisioned the new edition, and Matthew Cory of Element Books
revised and edited it. Irving Sunshine stood by patiently and

lovingly while the work was being done. To all these, I am exceedingly grateful.

I have relied heavily on the work of Quispel, Pagels, Hans Jonas, Bentley Layton, and Kurt Rudolph, among others, for important background material. To James Robinson, General Editor of *The Nag Hammadi Library*, and to all the team members of the Coptic Library Project of the Institute for Antiquity and Christianity, Claremont, California, who introduced to the English-speaking public the Gnostic texts found in Upper Egypt in 1945, I am especially indebted for their long and tireless labors, and for permission to use excerpts from the texts they have translated in this book. Bentley Layton's *The Gnostic Scriptures* provided me with information on additional Gnostic texts not found in *The Nag Hammadi Library*. If my interpretations do not coincide with their intent, I take full responsibility for any discrepancies.

JUNE SINGER
Pepper Pike, Ohio, 1999

FOREWORD

IN ANCIENT TIMES, SAILORS WERE the ones who cast out into unknown waters. We too have sudden eerie moments, months and seeming eons in our lives, that suddenly come upon us, and leave us feeling as though we are not casting off, but rather, drifting, or else held inert in dry dock. It is in such a time that we wish to receive into our hands, a book that would help to breathe new life into our sails gone dead from too much involuntary ennui and ambivalences about life. We wish almost more than anything else for words, images, that will re-animate our connections to the Divine. We long for that—"I know not quite what"— that will lift the bedraggled silver ship of soul up out of its dry dock, and compel it to slide back down again into fresh waters.

There is an ancient impulse in human beings who find themselves spiritually under-employed, who find it satisfying to be assigned a certain set of manners, a pride of gestures, a specific flock of prayers, and also to be assigned times to perform such. These ablutions, carried out consistently enough, become like the keeping of the log during a night sea journey, wherein the work is not only to sail, but also to take careful note of the present and coming weather, to assess the speed of navigation, to count the quality and the quantity of the stocks and stores of the ship of soul, as well as consulting with the instrument made famous by Tycho Brahe, the *sextans*, in order to scry that eternal timetable writ in the stars overhead. It is spiritual practice which not only nourishes, but also eases the vessel for the soul and psyche away from reefs and crags, where it can, so easily, be run aground and broken apart.

The syncopation of spiritual practices ought not to be looked upon as drudgery, but rather as the soulful rhythm of rest, and action, and rest again; as opportunity to regularly draw down the sails for mending, to regularly swim beneath the water line to inspect all rivets and shields, instead of acting as though the ship carrying the precious soul is invincible in its course, until its sails are so in tatters that they have become too tangled and threadbare to be easily repaired.

There is in all, a natural hunger towards spiritual renewal. In many present cultures—this natural longing for fresh spiritual food has become a malnutrition, and then an outright starvation. We desire a few illuminated words to teach us, to remind us how to tether the ship's "monkey-ego" on deck, not to let it steer the course, and how to derive from the ancient words, like those herein, the richest outcomes. In this book, you will find that what you are about to read are substantive, nourishing and time-tested riggings for your journey.

Knowledge of the Heart: Gnostic Secrets of Inner Wisdom is a Book of Hours. For the reader, for the seeker, who picks up this book and knows not much about books of hours, or the history and validity of these 'once were lost but now are found' gospels, Dr. Singer offers her knowledge of both.

She is, in her own words, a scribe—a centuries-old sacred calling—one who places ideas on parchment, or in modern times, CD-ROMs. She has gathered together in this book some of the important words and ideas which have had the strange history of appearing and disappearing over time according to the temperament of whichever over-culture currently presided. In this book, her work is fully evidenced with a fine scholasticism augmenting her training as a Jungian analyst. As compared to her previously published works, this one also maintains an honest, and mindful attitude.

The introductory chapter of this book is written as an unusually readable history of Gnosticism in relation to the early Church and its factions. Dr. Singer shows us the interactions between Judaism, the Gnostics, the Jewish Christians and the Gentile Christians, and presents us with a discernible picture of those times—and how the ideas, arguments and philosophies of that time affect us today. She gives us a feel for which ideas took on a life of their own and seemed to steadfastly refuse to be eliminated from the body of sanctioned literature, and lingered in wisps throughout oral traditions until some of the actual buried writings were rediscovered. It was *the people*, in effect, the lovers of God, who stubbornly refused to allow the stories of an eon to become extinct, no matter what or whichever council tried to impose its will alone.

It can be said truthfully that the Gnostics went underground to protect their rich and earthy direct knowledge of God, a relationship with the Divine that was without intermediaries or authoritative proscriptions. It is an understanding of this goodly history, this poetry, and the intent of these chosen readings that make this book a little gem.

Whether meditating at sunrise, or midday, or at night, or any of the offices in between, here are 'topics' to meditate upon, such as, "What Shall We Say of the Father?," or "If You Are Called," or "Discerning What is Before Your Eyes," or "The Opposites Within." Such daily disciplined practices bring the sacred *temenos* to bear on our often frenzied versions of "true life," one too often rife with ego pettiness, molehills made into mountains, inconveniences made into catastrophes. Prayer is meant to tame the storms created by clashes between ego and soul. Prayer is the story in which the soul always masters the storm: arriving in the beginning filled with desire, through the middle with great fervency, and all through to the end, transformed, triumphant.

Let this book give you the sense of allowing the wind to set your course, that is, go on the breath of The Great One, as it is said—in quiet waters, at certain hours of the sun and moon, in the tradition of all who have sailed—clad in monk's cloth, in shimmering veils, in robes rough woven, in shirts rubbed thin on the ropes, faces weathered, and eyes far seeing, of all those who prayed to remember that we are never—not even in the troughs and mountains of the greatest ravaging seas, we are never, ever, abandoned. The Greater, The Source without source, is *riding fo'c'sle*, that is, standing up on the topside forecastle deck near the prow, utterly commanding the course.

CLARISSA PINKOLA ESTÉS, Ph.D.

1NTRODUCTION

THE WORK OF THE SCRIBE

You see, O child, through how many bodies [elements],
how many ranks of demons, how many concatenations and
revolutions of stars, we have to work our way in order to
hasten to the one and only God?[1]

IN MY MIND'S EYE I SEE AN IMAGE of a scribe seated beside
a window that opens to the morning light. He wears a long
black robe with a hood draped around his shoulders. The sun's
rays fall across a slanted board in his lap as he transcribes those
ancient words onto the cured hide of a goat. I know, in some
way that I cannot explain, that I have been such a scribe. How
many lifetimes ago? Perhaps time and time again. Although
what I write today appears in letters of light beaming from a
cathode ray tube, then I wrote upon a palimpsest, a piece of
parchment scraped clean after each writing. Nevertheless some
impression of the past always remain to work its subtle effect
upon what will be written later. The mind is a palimpsest that
holds onto the imprint of the past, however faintly—even of the

cultures of past generations as transmitted by the elders through instruction, folklore and myth.

In the monastic tradition, a lector intones the sacred text while meals are eaten in silence. Then the scribe writes down what he has heard, but he can scarcely convey in his writing the sound of the words or the intonations of the reader's voice. "Writing" is a metaphor for communicating a stream of thoughts and feelings that really cannot be represented adequately when they are frozen in an unchanging format. Nor can thoughts be properly expressed in literal terms, for the "literal" is only a sequence of letters—black squiggles on a white page—which is then interpreted by different readers in their own individual ways.

I am not a theologian, a philosopher, or an exegete. As a modern scribe, I copy, shape and form manuscripts that are not my own. I cannot know for certain what those who framed them intended to convey, but I do have my own ideas about them. When I transcribe what was originally composed many centuries ago, I do it with careful attention to the order of the words and to their possible meanings. When passages do not quite make sense to me, I take the liberty of editing them for the sake of clarity. I freely admit that sometimes my attention is led away from the texts by my own curiosity. Maybe that is the same as my intuitive perception of those practically invisible messages lingering in the writing surface. I do not blanch when I read these words in Borges' story, "The Lottery in Babylon": "No book is published without some discrepancy in each one of the copies. Scribes take a secret oath to omit, to interpolate, to change. The indirect lie is also cultivated." My willingness to depart from the letter of the text may be based, at least in part, on my belief that in some inexplicable way we all have direct access to the past. We know things that we have never personally observed and have never been taught. We are permeable to the ideas of the past and, if we have enough openness and enough courage, we can allow ourselves to become vehicles for their expression. This is a task to which I commit myself.

I suspect that my own scribal history goes back as far as the 4th century BCE, after the Jews had returned to Palestine from their exile in Babylonia. Few of them could read; even fewer knew how to write. As long as they had remained in their homeland, priests had been their sole authorities in matters both secular and sacred. Priests had taught and interpreted to them the tenets of the Hebrew religion. Priests decided upon matters of ritual practice and moral behavior. Until the conquest of Jerusalem and the destruction of Solomon's Temple that stood on the Holy Mount, the Temple had been the only place where the worship of the God of Israel could be rightfully observed. The period of the Exile had been a time of deep sorrow for the Hebrew people: "By the rivers of Babylon, There we sat down, yea, we wept, when we remembered Zion."[2] Yet gradually, and perhaps out of an earlier Bedouin tradition which eventually found its way into mainstream Judaism, another belief emerged, that God must be with his people wherever they happened to be. Before the reign of King Solomon, God was *Immanuel* (God is with us). He was worshipped in a tabernacle, a tent that could be picked up and moved around as the people traveled from place to place.

This paradox—God is in his Temple/God is with us—was a source of deep theological debate during the Exile. During the time in Babylon the scribes began to write down the sacred literature which, until then, had been transmitted mostly through an oral tradition. A degree of democratization took place under the influence of the alien societies and governments, that opened the way to the greater acceptance of the scribe. Through his work the Holy Writ was made accessible to more of the people, instead of only to the priests. This shift slowly and almost imperceptibly compromised the pre-eminence of the priest. In time, the supremacy of learned argument prevailed over authoritative decree. It was then that the scribe began to take his rightful place in Judaeo-Christian history. And I, being of that lineage, feel a responsibility to clarify certain words before we go further into the mystery of certain sacred documents.

GNOSTICISM, GNOSTICS AND GNOSIS

GNOSTICISM

Gnosticism was one of the earliest and long-lived branches of Christianity. It was banned after the Roman Empire became Christianized in the 4th century when theological objections to Gnosticism were given the force of law. Gnosticism had reached its peak of activity during the first two centuries of the Common Era. While we now can read the writings of the Gnostics, we know very little about how literally or how symbolically they understood their texts or, for that matter, how the written word played out in their behavior. There are no standard interpretations of Gnosticism. Traces of the old beliefs exist in many places all over the world, in many guises and under many different names. But the religious beliefs of those who have adopted certain features of Gnosticism in our own time are not the same as those of the ancient past. Today, those in search of inner wisdom may find that the work of the ancient Gnostics points to important psychological (if not literal) truths. Today, understood metaphorically, contemplation of those secret books can lead us toward a more personal and intimate experience of the God within. This is the essence of *gnosis*.

GNOSTICS

Historically, "Gnostic" has two meanings. First, it refers to all the religious connotations in the Gnostic texts. Second, it refers to members of the ancient Christian sect called, in Greek, *gnostikoi*, Gnostics. There were certain sectarian features in the Gnostic mythology that distinguished the Gnostics as a group: 1) they had a complex and distinctive myth of origin; 2) they had a strong sense of group identity—they knew who had *gnosis* and who did not; 3) they used a special jargon or "in-group" language. For example, they did not refer to themselves as Gnostics, but they regarded their ancestors as spiritual proto-types,[3] and regarded themselves as the offspring, seed, posterity, or of the "race of Seth;"[4] 4) they had certain distinctive rituals and sacraments; and 5) they excluded from their writings any description of the ordinary life of the sect.

GNOSIS

Gnosis is a Greek word which means "to know". GNO is the Greek root of words like (K)NO or knowledge, Genesis, genetics, genealogy, gender—all of which relate to origins—another word with the same root. The word "gnosis" as we understand it today does not refer to ordinary knowledge, that is, knowledge received from some authority and consensually regarded as "the truth." Gnosis is revealed knowledge, or inner wisdom, that streams from a wellspring within the individual. It is more like *original* knowledge, that we are born with. One might say it is the natural essence of ourselves which has not been altered substantially by external influences.

Gnosis is a way of apprehending the world, that is not limited to the biases of any particular time or place. It is to be found not in the understanding of the mind, but in the sensibility of the heart. In its ancient form Gnosis was concerned with a radical dualism that envisioned an alien God who is transcendent to this universe, over and against the many gods and goddesses who were believed to reside in and to exercise a measure of control over the world we live in. The transcendent God, also called "Spirit," was said to be revealed through fragments of light that exist in human beings and which form a bridge between this world and the dwelling place of the Most High, whose realm is beyond the cosmos or any part of it that we are capable of exploring by rational (scientific) means. The knowledge that is thus revealed constitutes the whole of the Gnostic mythology, which reads everything in a direction opposite from orthodox theology; what is true in a limited world view is false in an unlimited world view; what is true in a closed system is false in an open system; and vice versa. Gnosis does not negate conventional wisdom; rather, it holds up to it a reflective glass that reveals the side which was hidden before. Thus gnosis can enable us to shift our perspective at will, to see that an individual life is brief and singular and therefore we would do well not to overvalue it. We fall like leaves from a tree, some early and some late, but the tree endures, and the forest even longer. This is a natural process. Time and eternity exist side by side; without one, the other would be meaningless.

A note about capitalization

I use the word "God" when speaking of the unknown, alien God of the Gnostic, and "god" to refer to the many gods and god images that are worshiped by various communities on earth. Likewise "Father" refers to the highest God, while "father" refers to earthly concepts. "Spirit," when capitalized refers to the Father, and "spirit" to that aspect in human beings which is drawn to seek the Divine. "Man," when capitalized, refers to the heavenly archetype after whose likeness the earthly Adam was fashioned, while "man" refers to human beings. "Gnosticism" is capitalized when referring to the religious practices of the several centuries before and after the time of Jesus. The people who lived in those times and observed the practices are called "Gnostics." "Gnosis," capitalized, refers to the special knowledge that was theirs. When using "gnosis" generically, as a kind of knowledge that may be experienced by all people in all ages, the word is not capitalized. Such words as "Thought," "Forethought," and "Truth," when referring to the special gifts of the highest God, will be capitalized, but when describing human qualities they will be in lower-case. In general, capitals will suggest the invisible world of the Gnostic, and lower-case will describe what belongs to our everyday lives in this mundane world.

A BRIEF HISTORY OF GNOSTICISM

IT IS PRACTICALLY IMPOSSIBLE TO WRITE an unbiased history of Gnosticism from the days of its flowering in late antiquity. All that we have at our disposal is hearsay evidence of what the Gnostic communities were like, how the people lived, and what their practices were, because the Gnostics themselves did not write about their own beginnings. They were not especially concerned with events as they occurred over time, for the temporal world was no more to them than a necessary way station, with its attendant trials and terrors, through which they had to pass on the way to their eternal home. Their "history," as they committed it to writing, is a true mythology, having no relation to external happenings but based upon their inner experiences of vision, fantasy or imagination that they projected onto both the visible, material world, and the invisible, spiritual world to which they claimed a special access. Added to this is the fact that religious experience for them was esoteric in nature, and they were loath to disclose its mysteries to those who were not fully committed to its mythos and initiated into its practices.

Although it has long been generally believed that Gnosticism is a variant or heretical form of Christianity which reached its zenith during the first and second centuries of the Common Era (CE), scholars now trace its origin to the many forms of Judaism extant between the time of the Babylonian exile and their return to Judah about fifty years later. If we are to appreciate the background that provided form and substance to Gnosticism at its inception, it is necessary to look at the religious and political situation among the Jews at that time, out of which many Gnostic concepts were conceived.

After the First Temple, built in the reign of King Solomon, was destroyed in 586 BCE, many Jews were taken into captivity in Babylon, while others dispersed throughout Elam, Assyria, Lower and Upper Egypt, the Greek islands, and elsewhere. Not all of the Jews were expelled from their homeland, for it was the policy of Nebuchadnezzar to exile the wisest and most powerful, and to permit the lesser Jews to remain. These lesser Jews, who then assumed power, neglected the laws of "purity" as a people and mingled with their conquerors, intermarrying with them and tolerating the worship of foreign gods and their images.

Among the exiles there were those who held fast to their Jewish faith and others who assimilated to themselves some of the beliefs and practices of the religions of the countries where they found themselves living. Especially in the Greek islands and in Egypt, many were exposed to Hellenistic ideas, and nowhere was this more evident than in the cosmopolitan city of Alexandria. Founded by Alexander the Great in 332 BCE, people of every land and every faith were drawn there, from the basin of the Tigris and Euphrates to the banks of the Nile.

In Babylonia during the Exile, the "Five Books of Moses" received their definitive form and the Torah became the moral essence of the Jewish religion. The Jews, scattered and leaderless, without the support of a state or a government of their own, were forced to find their own means of preserving their identity. As they turned to their records and their laws, their writings took on a new importance. From this time on we hear more of the scribes—earlier they had been mere secretaries, or clerks, but now they became an important caste, writing down the oral traditions, copying precious scrolls brought from the demolished Temple, and ordering and editing the Jewish archives. At the same time, ironically enough, the Hellenizing movement among Jews grew in strength. It was the Golden Age of Greek culture, when its sculpture, philosophy, poetry, and drama spread throughout the Mediterranean world.

The Babylonian empire fell to the Persians in 538 BCE. Unlike earlier imperial powers, who had been both intolerant and nationalistic, the ruling class of the Persians held to an ethical and universalistic faith. The Persian king, Cyrus the Great, was a Zoroastrian, believing in one eternal beneficent being,

"Creator of all things through the holy spirit." Cyrus himself may have instigated the return of the Jews to their homeland. Not all, but most of them did return, in several waves. The first two waves did not flourish. The third and fourth waves, under Ezra, "the Moses of the returning community," and Nehemiah, a diplomat and statesman as well as a man of action, succeeded in stabilizing the settlement. At first these leaders were shocked to find the degree to which the community of Jews who had remained had assimilated the customs and the culture of their neighbors. Regarding his co-religionists who had been left behind as a degenerate people, Ezra instituted harsh measures to bring about moral reform. He annulled intermarriages and broke up the alliances that had been formed through them. He reinstituted Temple worship, as well as *Kashruth* (the dietary laws) and circumcision. Yet there were still some Jews who continued to ally themselves with the foreign powers.

While many Jews were attracted to the Hellenizing movement, the orthodox Jews resisted it strenuously. Nevertheless, Jerusalem was converted into a city of the Greek type, and by 167 BCE the Syrian ruler, Antiochus Epiphanes, had made Hellenization compulsory. Antiochus, with a zeal that some writers say bordered on madness, attacked the adherents of the Mosaic Law by force of arms. He sought to substitute the cult of Olympian Zeus for the monotheistic religion of Judaism. He prohibited circumcision, the observance of the Sabbath, and other important Jewish practices as though they were criminal and corrupt customs.[5] This outrage led to civil war between the Maccabees, who fought to preserve the purity of the Temple and the faith, and the Hellenizers. The defenders of the Temple and of orthodoxy prevailed at that time, as the celebration of *Chanukah* commemorates, and the religious practices of the observant Jews were restored. Nevertheless, heterodox

Judaism continued to exist among Jews in Palestine and also among those who had moved away and settled in other parts of the eastern Mediterranean world.

Sources of Gnosticism other than Judaism have been suggested, among them older religions such as the Zoroastrian, Mesopotamian, and even the Indian religions. As the desert peoples of Egypt and the Near East turned their attention toward the great spaces above them, gazing at the stars and the wandering planets, they tended to regard these as powers that were malevolent rather than neutral or good. From them came the astrological elements that developed as symbols within Gnosticism. Other aspects of Gnosticism derived from late Hellenistic philosophy, especially incipient Neoplatonism with its concept of "archetypal ideas" that were thought to have preceded the establishment of material forms. And, finally, the heterodox Christian movements of those times were extremely important in the development of Gnosticism, bringing in such elements as millenarian predictions and their view of Jesus as the redeeming Messiah.

All these currents flowed together in the intellectually vibrant city on the Nile Delta. There were probably more Jews in Alexandria at that time than in Jerusalem. In a place where philosophers, rabbis, priests and priestesses, social commentators and teachers, lived in close proximity with one another, many groups formed around the more dynamic leaders: prophets and sages, self-proclaimed messiahs, and no small number of magicians and astrologers. Those who did not preach often wrote down the words of those who did, and thus a large body of literature came into being. Much of this material was contemporaneous with written reports about a certain Nazarene rabbi who had been preaching in and around Jerusalem and had acquired a remarkable following, especially among the "street people."

It was still the situation at the time of Jesus that the varieties of Judaism being practiced in Jerusalem and the countryside around raised many questions in the mind of Jesus and of other great Jewish teachers as to what really was "authentic Judaism." Jewish Gnostics were among those who deviated from the orthodox Temple tradition but still had a background in and considerable knowledge of Jewish tradition. By the end of the 2nd century CE, Gnosticism had become one of the three great religions in that region of the world, along with Christianity and Judaism.

Over the next two centuries, the new religion of Christianity gained more and more adherents. There were "Jewish Christians," who had been born Jews and had accepted the teachings and the messiahship of Jesus, and there were also the "gentile Christians," who had come from the many sects and religions in the ancient world to follow the teachings of the one who was called alternately the "Son of Man" and the "Son of God." Under Roman domination, the early Christians were persecuted for disagreeing with the reigning powers and their form of government. Consequently, many of them went underground and continued to exist as small sects, each with its own interpretation of the life and message of the Messiah. To add to the pluralistic character of the early Church in those first centuries, its adherents who came from so many and varied groups tended to graft the new religion onto the remnants of the older faiths. This created a pluralism that survived not only in ritual and practice, but also in the writings that emerged. The Gospels of Luke, Matthew and John were composed during the period from 70–100 CE, while the original form of the gnostic "Apocryphon of John" dates to about 100 CE. According to Professor Gilles Quispel, the "Apocryphon of John" is a Jewish work to which additions were made during the Christian era to establish the document as a revelation of the Savior to John while he was meditating in the desert.

When the Roman Emperor Constantine converted to Christianity in the 4th century, the "underground church" became the Imperial Church. The early Church fathers found it necessary to define the doctrines and to establish the creeds, the practices and body of literature which would characterize Christianity and Christianity alone, so that its devotees would know what they were expected to believe and how they were expected to behave. The actual setting forth of the basic dogma was done at Nicaea in 325 CE, on the basis of the recently closed canon of the New Testament. This accomplishment contributed to the institutionalization of the Church.

Along with institutions come hierarchies and authorities which determine what is and what is not acceptable with respect to belief and practice. Many of the writings of the Gnostics fell into the "not acceptable" category, since they vehemently opposed the establishment of any authoritative institution to which people should be expected look for moral guidance and spiritual instruction. As we will see from their original writings, the Gnostics were clear in their assertions that the gift of gnosis cannot be acquired through the services of an intermediary. With a firm conviction that the spark of the Divine rests within the individual human soul and can only be discovered through self-knowledge, the idea of a hierarchy that would pronounce on the validity of their direct experience was unacceptable to the Gnostics. Likewise, to a Church that was only in the first stages of the process of defining itself, the idea of a group of people determining individually, or in concert, the fate of their own souls was equally inadmissible.

Furthermore, among the Gnostic writings were some that gave special recognition to the Feminine. Perhaps these remained as traces of the lost feminine voice in Judaism, as suggested by Richard Elliott Friedman in his book, *Who Wrote the Bible?*, in which he gives evidence for the possibility that early "J" (Yahwistic) strands of the Hebrew Bible may have been written by a woman. Harold Bloom elaborates this theme in *The Book of J,* by pointing out the many references to the power and importance of the feminine in the "J" sections of the Bible, and asserts that the writer may even have been a member of the court of King Solomon. The prominence of the Feminine in Gnostic literature is also thought to have been derived from traces of the older oriental goddess worship that had found their way into the Bible. In any case, for the Gnostics the Feminine was an essential and dynamic aspect of the divine Unity. We will see, as we read excerpts from the gnostic tractates "Thunder: Perfect Mind," and "The Exegesis on the Soul," that the gnostic view of the Feminine was radically different from the Church's idealized image of Mary, whose prime function was to serve as a vessel for the incarnation of the masculine aspect of God.

In the conflicts that arose between the Church and the coexisting but dissenting sects, the Church was successful in establishing itself as preeminent. Other groups were discredited and even denounced as heretical and their adherents were often persecuted. Their writings were excluded, of course, when the New Testament was canonized. But the Gnostics had the foresight to go underground with their "aberrant" ideas, and they continued to meet in secret. They preserved their sacred books and hid some of them in caves in the Egyptian countryside, to await a time when the world might be more ready to receive them. The groups of Gnostics disappeared from public view, and all that was heard about them for many centuries was what could be found in the writings of the early Church fathers who recounted scurrilous rumors about their morality and roundly denounced their philosophy.

Nevertheless, the Gnostic myths persisted and the particular psychological approach to life that emerged out of their world view found other forms of expression. The core ideas of gnosis have been ever-present in the culture (or, perhaps one should say, the counterculture) of the West as a counterpoint to those of the major religions. Some of these ideas appear in the mystical writings of Judaism and her daughter religions, Christianity and Islam, where they describe ways in which ordinary people, as well as those specially gifted, experience the Divine presence in the world of the here and now. They surface as an emphasis on the dualism between the world of light above and the world of darkness and ignorance below, or they point to ways to support the tension of these opposites with a view toward reconciling these two worlds. It is beyond the scope of these brief notes to trace the many outcroppings of gnostic ideas through the centuries. Only a few names and dates will be noted here that will serve to anchor in our minds the invisible presence of gnosis as it persists through the centuries. Jewish esotericism was active during the first two centuries of the common era, with its *Merkabah* or "throne mysticism." These doctrines, concerning the ascent of the soul through many heavens and many hierarchies on its way to the divine presence, find an echo in parts of the gnostic mythology of the same period. Between 120 and 130 CE, many of the basic gnostic texts were written down on parchment and bound in leather volumes. The year 160 CE marks the death of Valentinus, founder of the important Valentinian school of Gnosticism which gave rise to such crucial gnostic texts as "The Gospel of Truth," "The Gospel of Philip," and "The Tri-Partite Tractate."

Gnostic and gnostic-like writing continued to appear. The prophet Mani, born in Babylon in 216 CE, received a call to be the "Apostle of Light." He founded the Manichean movement, based on the struggle of the forces of light against the forces of darkness. Manichaeism endured for at least a thousand years, spreading throughout the Middle East and as far east as China, where it was finally outlawed in 1120. In Bulgaria, from 920 on, a gnostic group that called itself the Bogomils (Beloved of God) was active. The 12th century was marked by the rise of the Cathars in Languedoc, Provence and Gascony. The Cathars believed that the devil worked through the powers and con-straints of the material world and they sought to free themselves from his influence. Between the crusade against the Cathars led by Louis VIII of France in 1226, and the last Cathar to be burned at Villerouge Termenes in 1321, Languedoc had come under the French crown and the Cathars disappeared from view. This is not to say that their ideas were lost or forgotten.

During the Italian Renaissance, Giovanni Pico della Mirandola wrote his *Oratio* as an introduction to the 900 Theses to be debated in Florence; and Giordano Bruno published his *De l'infinito universo e mondi* (On the infinite universe and worlds), both of which works were pronounced to be heretical because of their gnostic-like contents. Pico fled from his perse-cutors and died at the age of 31, and Bruno was burned at the stake as an "impenitent heretic."

The 17th and 18th centuries saw traces of Gnosticism surviving in such places as the *Rosicrucian Manifesto*, and in the formation in Europe of Lodges of Freemasons promising the illumination of cosmic mysteries, and other esoteric groups. Mozart's opera *The Magic Flute* is suggestive of gnostic rituals as they were adopted into Freemasonry—a society in which the composer held membership. In Germany, Jacob Boehme, a shoemaker and philosopher, wrote a vast array of intuitively gnostic works with strong affinities to Kabbalah, a mystical tra-dition within Judaism. In 1787, a 4th- or 5th-century gnostic manuscript, "Pistis Sophia," was discovered in Egypt, near Luxor, by James Bruce, and was placed in the British Museum. At the end of the 18th century and the beginning of the 19th, the English poet and painter William Blake issued his predominantly gnostic *Book of Urizen* and his epic poem *Jerusalem*. Blake had been strongly influenced by Boehme and most likely was familiar with "Pistis Sophia" as well. During the first half of the 20th century, gnostic scholars were translating, studying and interpreting the few gnostic works then extant. Leading among these were Gilles Quispel of Holland, Hans Jonas of Germany, and Jean Doresse of France. But most of what was commonly believed still about Gnosticism, came from teachings of the early Church fathers, who wrote diatribes against what they unequivocally called "heresies."

THE NAG HAMMADI LIBRARY

IN 1945, THERE CAME A MOMENTOUS event for Gnosticism and indeed for the whole of Western religious thought. It gave to the world for the first time an extensive collection of *original* gnostic works in the words of their authors. A long-buried collection of books was discovered at Nag Hammadi in Upper Egypt. Quispel and Doresse were among the first to recognize their significance. Well versed in the Coptic language, both of these men studied these original documents and urged their preservation and acquisition by responsible authorities who would make them available to scholars.

By an interesting coincidence between 1945 and 1947, not one, but two sets of ancient manuscripts—the Nag Hammadi Library and the Dead Sea Scrolls—came to light after having been hidden away for many centuries. These two bore certain parallels. Both had belonged to communities that stood at the fringes and took a critical view of the official religion of their time. The Dead Sea Scrolls that were found at Qumran on the shore of the Dead Sea depicted the lifestyle and belief structure of the Essenes over and against the Judaism of Jerusalem. In a cave in Egypt in the mountains south of Cairo, and equally significant, the original gnostic texts were found in some stone jars by peasants who were looking for fertilizer. The gnostic texts bore a relationship to orthodox Christianity of those times similar to that of the Dead Sea Scrolls to orthodox Judaism. Both collections of manuscripts had apparently been concealed at times of crisis and under external pressure. There are also certain points of agreement in their ideology, despite their differences. Both value a dualistic way of thinking and pose a negative view of this world against a hope for redemption in the world to come, either after a victory of the sons of light over the denizens of darkness or through the liberation of a divine spark or the soul. The histories of both documents, between their discovery and their coming to public attention, are veiled in mystery and intrigue, but it is with the Coptic Gnostic texts and some of their implications for our own lives today that we are concerned in this book.

The discovery of the cache of 52 books that had been hidden since the 4th century of the Common Era in a mountain cave in the desert evoked the interest and excitement of explorers, scholars, and dealers in Egyptian antiquities. The circumstances of the discovery were fascinating in themselves, but even more so when elaborated in the fashion of Oriental storytelling. The men who found the books could not read, but they saw how old the manuscripts were and thought they might be of some value if they sold them to the merchants and collectors who sometimes came around looking for ancient artefacts. In 1946, Togo Mina, the Curator of the Egyptian Museum in Cairo, was said to have purchased an incomplete and damaged papyrus codex for 250 Egyptian pounds from a Coptic teacher from the region of Nag Hammadi. Togo Mina showed his new acquisition to two French orientalists, Henri Corbin and François Daumois, who were able to establish the Gnostic character of the document. They planned to publish an edition the following year. Meanwhile, another Frenchman, Jean Doresse, was also informed of the discovery by Togo Mina. As soon as he read a few passages, Doresse recognized the great importance of the codex and undertook a more complete investigation.

Soon after, another portion of the Nag Hammadi find surfaced, and this was offered to the Bollingen Foundation in New York and the Bibliothèque Nationale in Paris—both without success. Neither group understood the value of the codices. Then the Dutch church historian, Professor Gilles Quispel, took over the task of mediator in the negotiations for its purchase. Dr. Quispel has told me how he had managed to locate the first codex, the whereabouts of which had been sealed in secrecy since its discovery. With the help of the famous and influential psychologist, Carl Gustav Jung, Quispel was able to locate and then to negotiate the purchase of the first codex. Traveling from Cairo back to Europe, he was asked by the customs official what he was carrying in that package under his arm. "Just some old books," Quispel replied nonchalantly, and he was passed through the gate.

When word got out that these texts contained material that had been composed concurrently with literature that eventually became part of the New Testament, many people were extremely eager to gain access to it. They wanted to be able to learn for themselves what was in the books and why they had been excluded from those that were accepted as Holy Scripture. Then began many years of bickering among scholars and others over who would possess the translation rights and who would be the eventual owner of the manuscripts. Scholarly rivalries and the political situation in Egypt in the years following the discovery, hindered work on the manuscripts. In the 20 years after 1945, only a small portion of the texts had been edited and translated. This work was done mostly by European scholars. Less than 10 percent of that was available in English.

In 1966, the team responsible for the publication of *The Nag Hammadi Library* in English began to come together under the auspices of The Institute for Antiquity and Christianity, Claremont, California. The Director of the Institute, Professor James Robinson, put together a team of scholars, the members of the Coptic Gnostic Library Project of the Institute at Claremont, California. It was their task to assemble the fragments, translate them, and introduce them with appropriate commentaries. Robinson had long urged the publication in English of the entire Nag Hammadi Library. After careful and extended preparation, the definitive new translation was finally completed and was then published by Harper & Row in 1988. Now, for the first time, a very large and representative corpus of original gnostic writings was made available in English, and it was no longer necessary to depend upon the critiques of Gnosticism from the Early Church heresiologists. The accessibility today of the original texts translated from the Coptic into English allows readers to judge for themselves the merit and contemporary relevance of the ideas that have been hidden for so long.

The Gnostic Scriptures, by Bentley Layton, is another important basic reference on Gnosticism that saw publication at about the same time as *The Nag Hammadi Library*. Professor

Layton labored over the Coptic texts in Cairo for more than seven years, to produce an accurate and beautifully written new translation with annotations and commentary. His book includes the texts discovered at Nag Hammadi, other writings considered to be Gnostic, and some related writings. Layton's work is particularly valuable in that it is accessible to the reader who may not have a background in classical languages and theology.

ABOUT THIS BOOK

IT IS FROM SOME OF THE EXTRA-CANONICAL manuscripts in *The Nag Hammadi Library* and *The Gnostic Scriptures*, that I have selected the texts for *The Knowledge of the Heart*. They appealed to me because of their powerful ideas, of special relevance to our own times. As a psychologist and a Jungian analyst, I have been particularly attentive to the way they illuminate our own psychological processes. Many of these texts are mythological in nature. I understand myths such as these to be the language of the soul, or psyche, giving expression to the psychological processes that accompany life's crucial and transformative experiences. It is through myth that cultures, as well as individuals, reflect their inner reactions to external events. When faced with awesome mysteries, it is in the nature of human consciousness to make an attempt to explain rationally why things are as they are or why events occur as they do. Our sight is often so myopic that a kind of narrative is the best we can do. The storyteller tries to explicate something that comes alive in the telling, and the scribe tries to preserve the insight by writing it down.

Often people do not recognize these stories as myths. Sometimes we mistake them for falsehood, superstition, or the products of ignorance. This is especially true when they are someone else's myths and not our own, while, conversely, we often mistake our own mythology for objective fact. But I contend that the myths are true expressions of our inner selves, revealed cryptically in image, symbol, and metaphor. They are something like dreams: rationally they may not ring true, but in a *psychological* sense they are; they express people's inner processes through the use of ingenious devices that conceal what must be concealed and reveal what may be revealed.

I read the gnostic writings as expressions of the timeless longings of the human soul to penetrate the mysteries of existence. In every age and in every discipline of art or science, human beings seek answers to the same eternal questions that are found in an ancient formula ascribed to the great gnostic teacher, Valentinus:

Who am I?
What have I become?
Whereunto have I been thrown?
Whereto do I speed?
Wherefrom am I redeemed?
What is birth, and what rebirth?

However far we try to penetrate these questions with the intellect, sooner or later we come up against the dark veils of mystery. Yet the sparks shine through, like stars in the midnight sky. They beckon to us as they beckoned to our ancestors through the generations. In a time before time was measured, words were the garment of primal thought. Today it is through words that we redeem and illuminate the residues of these primal thoughts that they may bring light into our own lives.

A BOOK OF HOURS

K NOWLEDGE OF THE HEART IS DESIGNED as a Book of Hours, a traditional daily plan for meditative practice. The primary purpose of the book is to maintain awareness of the presence of the divine mystery within the sphere of the everyday world. Over the centuries, books of hours have been used most often by laity and monastics. They are structured around eight required periods ("offices") of prayer and meditation.

Midnight (*Matins*, or *Nocturnes*, as it is sometimes called) is said during the night some time around midnight, when the supplicant arises from sleep and prays from an inner space that is between the mundane and the eternal worlds.

Sunrise (*Lauds*, the first office of the day), is a meditation said at daybreak and welcomes the Light of the World.

Early morning (*Prime*) marks the conscious entrance into the activities of the day.

Mid-morning, Midday and Afternoon (*Terce*, *Sext* and *None*) are "the little hours," because they come during the working day, often in the field or the kitchen. They are brief pauses in the labor and are designed to remind the person that all work is done in the service of God.

Sunset (*Vespers*) is particularly important because, according to tradition, the new day begins with the setting of the sun on the old.

Night (*Compline*), may have been added by St Benedict for the purpose of helping the monks to settle down for the night. It comes at a time when we let go of daily concerns and enter into the darkness and its mysteries.

Meditations at Midnight

The God of old is dispossessed of his terrestrial empire, and every thinking being on this globe disdains him or knows him not. But what matter that men should no longer be submissive to Yaldabaoth, if the spirit of Yaldabaoth is still in them; if they, like him, are jealous, violent, quarrelsome and greedy, and the foes of art and beauty? What matter if they have rejected the ferocious demiurge? It is in ourselves and in ourselves alone that we must attack and destroy Yaldabaoth.

Anatole France, *The Revolt of Angels*

ℱIRST THOUGHTS—MATINS

The prophet saith: "At midnight I rise to praise thee, because of thy righteous ordinances."

Psalm 119:62.

THE CYCLE OF HOURS BEGINS in the deepest, darkest part of the night, when we are adrift in the limitless sea of the unconscious. We hear a bell, a call, and we are roused from our slumber. It is cold; we are weary and disoriented from sleep, not sure in which world we are. It is a time of slow and gradual emergence from the absolute blackness in which we have been so lately immersed.

Once there was a time when nothing was. Mind of all minds was asleep. How did Original Consciousness become aware of itself? This is the first great riddle that ever confounded human consciousness and it confounds us still. If the "cosmos" is an orderly, systematic universe extending far beyond our terrestrial sphere, and if astrophysicists today begin to speak of the form and shape of this universe and its limits, we must continue to ask: What lies beyond the stars, and in whose arms is matter enfolded? And how, and why, did the celestial lovers conceive in their non-material minds the possibility of a cosmos? And, if they were whole and complete in themselves, lacking nothing, how did it come about that their offspring is flawed? Such questions make little sense as we go about our activities in the course of every day, but in the darkest hours of the night it seems fitting to ponder them.

Followers of the traditional Judaeo-Christian religions have regularly assumed that a good god created the world we know, and that it is human beings, or the devil, who have made it less than the creator-god intended it to be. Perhaps they assert this for fear of offending the creator-god who, as they believe, has power of life and death over them. But there have always been those who took exception to the rule. Even in ancient times, the Gnostics refused to take all responsibility for the evil that exists in a world that supposedly was created by a god who is essentially good. They envisioned other possibilities in their mythology, so it is little wonder that their convoluted tales were often regarded by the Early Church Fathers as heretical. If we, however, can look at these myths as expressions of people's inner lives rendered in the language of the soul, we may find in them material for contemplation in a time out of time, when night allows us access to obscure mysteries.

The texts for Matins are taken from "The Apocryphon of John." "Apocryphon" means "secret writings." Despite its name, "the Apocryphon of John" (a disciple of Jesus) is thought to be a work of Jewish Gnosticism. It contains no Christian elements except for the introduction, the ending, and some minor interpolations indicating that the vision was revealed by the resurrected Christ. These elements were probably added later to the original text by a Christian redactor, but the vision itself is a Gnostic reinterpretation of the early chapters of Genesis. The book is believed to have been written in Alexandria about the beginning of the Christian Era by a group of Jewish dissidents who taught the existence of two gods, the Unknown God and a second god, His representative, sometimes called an angel or archangel, to whom all the anthropomorphisms of the Old Testament are applied. These Jews had been reared to believe that every word of the Bible was true and that God was one, yet the circumstances of their lives and of the world gave them cause to rebel against their inherited legacy. Some of these came to the gnostic solution, that indeed God is one and the Bible contains truth, but the personalistic character of a creator and a lawgiver belongs to a subordinate deity or angel.

Today, when we consider the persistence in our world of such evils as starvation in the shadow of luxury apartments, continuing production of weapons for mass destruction, and dreadful diseases flourishing because of the lack of money for treatment or cure, we may well reflect upon the sources of evil and the possibility of redemption from them, as symbolized in these ancient, yet still relevant, writings.

ENTERING THE DESERT

"Where is your master whom you followed?" a Pharisee said to me.
"He has filled your ears with lies, he has closed your heart,
    and turned you from the tradition of your fathers."

When I, John, heard these words, I fled the Temple;
I withdrew to the desert, grieving greatly, and I cried aloud,
"How then was the savior appointed, and why was he sent to us,
    by his Father? And what did he mean when he said to us,
'The realm to which you shall go is imperishable'?"

While I sat contemplating these things, lo, the heavens opened
    and the world shook and trembled beneath my feet!
In the light I beheld a youth who stood beside me.
Even as I looked he became like a old man, then like a servant.
Yet there were not three before me, but one, with multiple forms
    appearing through each other as though transparent.
He said to me, "John, John why do you doubt?
And why are you afraid? I am the one who is with you always.
    I am the Father. I am the Mother. I am the Son."

"The Apocryphon of John," *NHL*, pp. 105-6[6]

JOHN, HIS FAITH SHAKEN, FORSAKES the Temple and retreats to the desert. The Temple had been for him the fortress of his faith, the crown of Jerusalem, the place where he prayed, consorted with his friends, and found his identity as a man and as a Jew. Often he sat there at the feet of his teacher, drinking wisdom from his mouth. Leaving the City meant leaving the world John had always known, with its institutions and its rules, its prescriptions for behavior and thought and belief. Entering the desert means confronting the awesome mystery of the parched and rocky wilderness, alone, bereft of solace.

So it may be at times with us in the darkest hours of the night, or in the dark night of the soul when we doubt whatever we may have believed and even doubt ourselves, that we leave "the city" and find ourselves in "the desert." What made sense to us, what worked effectively for us in the bright day of consciousness, now dissolves in the shades of night. We peer into the invisible world, seeking answers to the questions we have avoided during the day. Now we face that from which all our activities have distracted us. When we awaken to find ourselves in that desert of the night, we are like the monks or hermits who arose from their slumbers at midnight to ask the ancient and eternal questions: "Who am I? What have I become? Whereunto have I been thrown? Whereto do I speed? Wherefrom am I redeemed? What is birth, and what rebirth?"

All of us, when we turn within, wonder about the meaning of life and, more exactly, the meaning of our own lives. We cannot deduce this meaning using intellectual knowledge alone, for that sort of knowledge can only tell us what something is, not what it means. For the latter, another kind of intelligence is needed, knowledge the of the heart, or gnosis. Gnosis means "insight," in the special sense of being able to see through all the varied layers of apparent reality into the very essence.

The "teacher" who appears to John comes to teach him what is, what was, and what is yet to be. He is visible but has no substantiality. He is transparent. We may understand him as a symbol for the mystagogue who is outside of ourselves and yet within us, the one who comes to us in the empty space created by our solitude and who teaches us to perceive what is, to remember what was, and to envision what is yet to come.

MORE THAN A GOD

I asked to know about these things, and he said to me:
"The Monad[7] is a kingdom with nothing above it.
The invisible One exists as God, and Father of every thing.
He is above every thing, existing as incorruption,
    shining forth as pure light into which no eye can look.

"It is not right to think of him as a god,
    for he is more than a god.
He does not exist in that which is inferior to him
    since every thing exists in him.
He is eternal, since he is lacking in nothing.
He is without limitation,
    since no one was prior to him to set limits for him.
He is unsearchable, since no one was prior to him to examine him.
There are no words to express his magnitude or his qualities
    for no one can know him."

The "Apocryphon of John," *NHL*, p. 106

THERE ARE GODS[8] AND THERE IS GOD. These are not the same. There are many gods, the gods of the Greeks and of the Romans, gods of the Aztecs and the Incas, gods of Sumer and Babylon, of Persia and India, of China and Japan, of Australia and Africa, gods of the Muslims, the Christians, and the Jews. All of these are tribal gods to the degree that they belong to a particular people and a particular people belongs to them. Battles are fought in the names of the gods, and the gods are invoked for the purpose of establishing a collective morality for a certain group. Some of their adherents seek political power, even in secular states, and divine will is often invoked in public ceremonies.

To one who has gnosis, these gods appear as creations of human beings who fashion them in their efforts to explain the inexplicable questions about their beginnings, as they seek protection from their enemies, and as they long for one to whom they can appeal for whatever they need or desire. Having been created, these gods take on a life of their own: they create a realm, a people, and rules by which these are governed; and the people come to believe that their god is *the* God. But gnostics say that they are mistaken, that while the many peoples of the many realms fight about which god is the true God, the God of Truth—who exists beyond the stars and beyond the farthest reaches of the cosmos—remains unknown, because this God has not been created either by the human intellect or by any other god. They speak of an alien God, mysterious, awesome, and unknowable through the limited minds of men and women. They say that God is immeasurable light, which is pure, holy, and immaculate.

We could as soon scoop up the ocean in a teacup as encompass the mind of God in our own understanding. Yet, if we are not blinded by the darkness of ignorance or constrained by the narrowness of our vision, we know that God exists, that God is One, and that through our inner wisdom we may come to an awareness of God, the One in whom every thing exists.

THE WOMB OF EVERY THING

The invisible Spirit looks at himself
  in the light that surrounds him, the water of life.
He gives to every realm in every way,
  putting his desire into the spring of the pure-light water.
His thought performed a deed, and she came forth:
  she appeared before him in the radiance of his light.
Her light shines like his light,
  the perfect power of the virginal Spirit.
She is the First Power to come forth from his mind.
She is the Forethought of the All.

She became the womb of every thing, for she is prior to them all:
  the Mother–Father, the first Man, the Holy Spirit,
  and the eternal realm among the invisible realms.
He looked at her with the pure light and she conceived from him.
He begot a spark of light and anointed it
  until it became perfect with the goodness of the Spirit.
When it had received from the Spirit,
  it glorified the Spirit and the perfect Forethought
  for whose sake it had come forth.

"The Apocryphon of John," *NHL*, p. 107

IN THE BEGINNING IS ONENESS, undifferentiated unity. All exists within the One, and the One nourishes the all. But the One is more than existence, it is also consciousness. It has desire and thought, and these act to separate the One into the two. The primal unity is broken when the First Thought comes forth. She is female. We are told that nothing can occur in the world of time and space until the feminine, whose attribute is forethought (*pronoia*), or intuition, is activated. Without this ability to look forward, to imagine, nothing can be conceived. The feminine principle is the active one, drawing forth the spark that will beget life from the One who is unbegotten. But for this life to be perfect, that is, whole, it is necessary that both the desire of the masculine principle and the receptivity of the feminine principle be in accord with one another.

What the ancient Gnostics regarded as the eternal invisible realm may be a distant prototype for the realm of the human unconscious. As embryo, we grow in the womb in a state of undifferentiated unity with our mother; but as child, we cannot go on living in this way. Our conscious life begins only at the moment of separation, when there is not one, but two—one's self and the other. We come into being physically as male or as female, but psychologically and spiritually we are androgynous: being and doing, masculine and feminine, capable of expressing any or all of the qualities of the essence that has been embedded in our genes from the beginning and transmitted through all the aeons of the generations. Often we forget that this potential exists within us, and we identify with our biological sex more than with our psycho/spiritual androgyny. It is then that the masculine aspect and the feminine aspect come into conflict and we find ourselves supporting the one and rejecting the other.

Perhaps this was why, when the disciples asked Jesus when they would enter the kingdom, he answered them: "When you make the two one, and when you make the outside like the inside, and the inside like the outside, and the above like the below, and when you make the male and the female one and the same so that the male not be male nor the female female ... then will you enter the kingdom." ("The Gospel of Thomas" (22), *NHL*, p. 129.)

Though it is clear enough that as physical beings we are either male or female, we are told here that in our essence and in our spiritual lives there is no difference between female and male, for each of us carries the spark of the divine in which male and female are united as a single one.

FIVE GIFTS OF THE FATHER

She, First Thought, requested from the invisible virginal Spirit
> to give her Foreknowledge,
> and when he had consented, Foreknowledge came forth.
She requested again that he grant her Indestructibility.
When he consented, Indestructibility came forth
> and it stood by Thought and Foreknowledge.
She requested once more that he grant her Eternal Life,
> and the invisible Spirit consented.
She requested again, to grant her Truth.
> and when he consented, Truth came forth.

All these attended and glorified the invisible Spirit
> and his feminine aspect,
> the one for whose sake they had come into being.

"The Apocryphon of John," *NHL*, p. 107–8

THESE FIVE ENDOWMENTS—Thought, Foreknowledge, Indestructibility, Eternal Life, and Truth—comprise what the Gnostics called the "pentad of the realms of the Father." Its qualities describe the character of the invisible world and differentiate it from the material or visible world. The invisible world of the Father is a world of ideals or *absolutes*, that shine as beacons before us, yet remain forever beyond our reach. In contrast, the qualities of the visible world are relative, that is, they are to be found in varying degrees of nearness as they are measured against the values of the other world. This gnostic "dualism," in its basic and essential form, posits an ideal world which we cannot understand simply by using the tools of the human intellect, and an actual world in which we live and which many people believe is the only reality.

In an ideal world where there is no time or space, there can be no difference between thought and deed; whereas here in the visible world we know so well, thought usually precedes action—though action does not always follow thought. Foreknowledge, also, is an absolute in the invisible world for the same reason: when every potential is present, the future is as easily accessible as the past. And so with Eternal Life: there can be no "degrees of eternity." Indestructibility is a quality of permanence. Finally, Truth, in the realm of the Father, is absolute. While in our everyday existence we may perceive fragments of truth and believe our truth to be the whole truth, the gnostic regards the many little truths as being like so many tribal gods—useful implements in a practical world but incomplete when viewed under the aspect of eternity.

The pentad of the realms of the Father is androgynous, with every being having its masculine and feminine aspect. The highest God and his First Thought comprise the double aspect of the virginal Spirit. From this syzygy, two light-beings emanate: the only begotten Son, and the Sophia. The human spirit reiterates this double aspect. The meaning of the Son for us is "logos," or "the word." The meaning of the Sophia is "wisdom," the eternal female, the archetype behind the great goddesses of the distant past and behind the re-emerging feminine principle in our own time. Now, as in antiquity, the Sophia claims the power that is rightfully hers because she received the divine light of the invisible virginal Spirit and First Thought.

To our inner wisdom she is distinctively feminine, regardless of our gender. Our feminine wisdom values truth more than information, permanence more than change. It is she in us who desires to see things whole, to see into things, to be able to anticipate and then to wait. When we are in touch with her we take the long view and are not seduced by expediency.

HOW THOUGHT BROUGHT
FORTH IGNORANCE

The Sophia conceived a thought from herself
    and the conception of the invisible Spirit
    and Foreknowledge.
She wanted to bring forth a likeness out of herself
    without the consent of the Spirit, her consort.
Because of the invincible power which is in her
    her thought did not remain idle.
Although the person of her maleness had not approved,
    yet she brought forth.
When she cast her eyes upon the consequence of her desire
    it took on the form of a lion-faced serpent
    with eyes like lightning fires which flash!
Seeing that it did not resemble her likeness, she cast it away,
    for she had created it in ignorance.
She surrounded it with a luminous cloud;
    she placed a throne for it in the middle of the cloud,
    that none of the immortals might see it save the holy Spirit
    who is called "the mother of the living."
And she called its name "Yaldabaoth."

"The Apocryphon of John", *NHL*, p. 110

WHEN THE FEMININE PRINCIPLE is balanced by the
masculine principle in a person, the visionary mind is
rooted in rational consciousness. But one without the other,
imagination without reason, leads us away from the light. When
the feminine becomes aware of her wisdom, she wishes to assert

her independence. Her gifts have endowed her with power, but she has yet to learn judgment, that is, discernment. She does not realize that she cannot withdraw from her union with the Father without incurring the consequences of the separation. The very potency of the feminine leads her into thought and this becomes action which, in turn, results in a monstrous demiurge instead of the wished-for perfect child. This creature, this misbegotten offspring, contains within itself all the fiery power of the mother and her willfulness as well. Although the mother, Sophia, is the symbol of archetypal wisdom, her wisdom has nevertheless to be tested and refined in the cauldron of experience before it will be able to stand up in the world of form. Wisdom begins with the recognition of the flaw in oneself.

When the Sophia sees what she has brought forth, she is ashamed and embarrassed, for her issue has not met her secret expectations. She casts it away, but she cannot utterly destroy it since she bears responsibility for it. She attempts to hide it from all of the immortals, yet she knows that she can hide nothing from the holy Spirit, since she herself exists in the divine androgynous Mother–Father.

In each human being, wholeness is represented by the archetype of the androgynous Self. The concept of the Self is as old as the Upanishads. In our own time, Jung called the Self "the central archetype of the psyche," which embraces both its conscious and unconscious aspects. Being androgynous, the Self contains all the pairs of opposites, such as light and dark, good and evil, masculinity and femininity. In our essential Self, in the fullness of our being, each of us possesses all the potencies of the twin aspects of the archetype. Were we all-wise, we would always choose the better aspect of the archetype as a guide for our behavior, but alas, our archetypal nature provides that we are at once wise and ignorant, and we must forever steer a cautious course between the opposites within.

In the myth, the error of Sophia results in the appearance of Yaldabaoth and his eventual dominion over the visible world. If her error was pride, his chief quality was envy, the natural consequence of pride. For pride demands that we be superior to others, and envy acknowledges that we are not.

THE THEFT OF THE LIGHT

Yaldabaoth stole power from his mother, for he was ignorant,
   thinking that there existed no other except his mother alone.
He became strong, and created numerous realms for himself
   with a flame of luminous fire which still exists.
Seven kings he placed over seven heavens, and five over the abyss.
He shared his fire with them, but not the power of the light
   which he had received from his mother,
   for he, the first archon, is ignorant darkness.
Each of the other archons created seven powers for themselves,
   and each of the powers created angels for themselves.

When the Arrogant One saw the creation which surrounds him
   and the multitude of angels which had come forth from him,
   he exalted himself above these and said to them:
"I am a jealous God and there is no God beside me."
By announcing this, he demonstrated to the angels who attend him
   that there exists another God.
For if there were no other, of whom would he be jealous?

"The Apocryphon of John," *NHL*, p. 110–12

YALDABAOTH IS THE CREATOR AND ruler of the visible
world, but the gnostic does not confuse him with the highest
God. Yaldabaoth is called "the chief archon"[9] and, as such, he has
qualities. He acts. He and his angels are subject to the passions
of the created world, which they then transmit to the creatures
of this world. The seven kings that Yaldabaoth placed over the
heavens refer to the planets, and their planetary spheres that

revolve around the earth are the "seven heavens" of ancient cosmology. To each is assigned a day of the week. The eighth sphere, beyond these, is the realm of the gods and angels. It is also the place where the Sophia is said to be at rest.

When the invisible Sophia looks down upon the impiety of the chief ruler, she cries out, "You are mistaken, Samael," that is, "blind god." Through her wisdom she offers to all humanity hope in a higher God above the jealous one. She says: "An immortal Man of light has existed before you and will appear among your modelled forms; he will trample you to scorn as a potter's clay is pounded. At the consummation of your works, all the defects that Truth has made visible will be abolished as though they had never been."

The realm of the Father lies beyond the created world, beyond the stars, even beyond the cosmos. Although the cosmos, or the "universe" as we call it, may be in large measure unknown, it still belongs to the knowable. Scientists today are investigating the limits of the universe, its shape and size, how it began and how it will end; as though someday we might know the answers to these questions. But the realm the gnostics call "beyond the stars" is unknowable. Since it has neither beginning nor end we cannot describe it by a list of qualities because these would limit it. Gnostics are aware of its existence, but cannot say anything about it except through the use of metaphor and symbol which act to link human consciousness with the mystery of the unknowable.

Endowed with the wisdom of the mother, Yaldabaoth "knows" of the higher God, but he does not know that he knows. He has knowledge but he does not have access to his knowledge; therefore he is ignorant. His plight resembles our own human condition when we do not have gnosis. Then we only believe what we see, or what has been proven to our satisfaction. Since it does not occur to us that we may be endowed with supernal wisdom, we do not open ourselves to the mystery of the Spirit that invisibly permeates the created world. So long as we limit our explorations and activities to the visible world as though that were all that existed, we must remain blind to the transcendent beauty of the eternal world.

SOPHIA'S PRAYER OF REPENTANCE

When the light of the Sophia had mixed with the darkness,
    it caused the darkness to shine.
But when the darkness of the archon had mixed with the light,
    it became neither dark nor light, but dim.
Then the mother began to move to and fro,
    aware that the brightness of her light had diminished.
When she saw the wickedness of what had happened,
    the theft of her light-power which her son had committed,
    she recalled that her consort had not agreed with her.
And she repented, with much weeping.

The powers of the invisible world, the whole pleroma,[10]
    heard the prayer of her repentance.
They offered praise to the invisible Spirit on her behalf.
When he had consented, it was not her consort who came to her,
    but the Son, in order that he might correct her deficiency.
And she was taken up, not to her own realm but above her son,
    to be in the ninth until she has corrected her deficiency.

"The Apocryphon of John," NHL, p. 111–13

WHAT IS THIS LIGHT THAT CAUSES "the darkness to shine"? It is the special wisdom of gnosis, the knowledge of an invisible reality. A result of the impulse of Sophia is that she has infused the world of creation with light from beyond the stars. Sparks of this light are scattered about through this world as the lost fragments of a past enveloped in eternity—silent and mysterious. Yet now and again they give evidence of their presence among us.

When the darkness of the archon mixes with the light, it causes the light to dim. Light is absorbed into the clouds of envy and ignorance. The ruler of the visible world and his legions are governed by their passions, and by these they mean to govern the human race. Imperfection gives rise to imperfection as the imperfect gods of tribes and of nations strive to impose their will upon the creatures who serve them, and to conquer those who will not.

Sophia, being all-wise, recognizes what is and what will be in the world of Yaldabaoth. She understands that the theft of wisdom does not make the thief all-wise, since he mistakes the part for the whole and thinks of himself as the only wise one. Desolate in her realization that she has been at fault through not securing the agreement of her consort, she sees that the garment of darkness now covering the world has come into being because of her single-mindedness. Dejected, despondent, forlorn and melancholy, she cries aloud to the very powers of the invisible world that she has abandoned. They hear her prayer of repentance, and respond. Have we not, each of us, at some time tasted bitterly of failure? The most tragic failure of all is the failure to recognize our truest self, to hear its voice, and to allow it to guide us where we are meant to go. How easily we forget the spark that burns within us, urging us to become what we are capable of being! We cover its light with a shroud of darkness and ignorance, until we no longer remember that it exists. In time the light dims, and many of us pass through our lives unaware of its presence. But if we awaken soon enough from the sleep of forgetfulness, whether stirred by melancholy, sickness, or grief, or simply touched by the grace of insight, we may still be able to set our feet on the path that leads toward gnosis, toward the sure knowledge of the indwelling invisible Spirit.

MEDITATIONS AT SUNRISE

At daybreak the monks rose and
prayed, "That we may be transfigured
by the rising sun." This is according
to the Rule of St Benedict.

ℱIRST THOUGHTS—LAUDS

The Prophet saith: "Seven times a day have I given praise to thee."

Psalm 119:164

O N AWAKENING, WE WHO HAVE PLACED ourselves at the service of consciousness recognize the dawn's early light as kin to the light that shines within us. As it grows brighter it dissipates the darkness and our tendency to sleep. Its warmth beckons us to move forward into the morning and whatever it may bring.

There is the light of day that shines upon us from the rising sun and there is the Light within the light, that rouses us from the sleep of oblivion and dissolves the last vestiges of our drowsiness. Refreshed now, we offer these prayers in praise of the light that grows more intense with every passing moment. This glorious light is able to clothe our every act with incandescence, if only we will allow it.

Light has two qualities: it is of transparent clarity, and it is reflective. In and of itself, light cannot be seen, yet without it no one can see anything. Light is always present to some degree, but when it is *visibly* present, worlds are unveiled before our eyes. Yet the question arises, do we really see a visible world, or do we only see light as it is reflected from the surfaces of objects?

Artists have always known that it is possible to create an image on canvas simply by placing side by side colors that reflect the light in different ways. Through light, a flat surface acquires depth and things are seen which do not exist. We have seen how the Impressionists dared to dissolve the boundaries of their images, so that we could no longer depend upon recognizable forms but had to construct the forms out of the tiny dots of brilliant color that made the light dance and play. Seen this way, light lets our minds leap from point to point without restraint like gazelles on a rocky slope.

Is it any wonder that since the beginning of recorded time people have always associated the highest God with light? For it was their perception that God, like light, is real but has no substance. God, like light, is present, but we cannot see it; yet without it we cannot see at all. God, like light, is indescribable; yet without it we can describe nothing for we are like blind people, groping about in a world of darkness. Only we do not speak here of literal blindness. We do not only mean those whose eyes cannot see outward, but blindness stands also for those individuals who cannot see inward, that is, with insight. To see only form and not to see meaning is blindness, and it is this blindness that the morning prayers at Lauds seek to dispel. Words that are uttered then, and psalms that are sung may penetrate into the very nature of that which light illumines, the nature of the One whom we call Father. Light reveals what was hidden and secret.

Therefore, how better, to welcome the dawn, than to raise our hearts in exaltation of the power that shines upon us from above and transfigures the ordinary tasks of the day, making of them acts of gratitude for the Light of our lives!

WHAT SHALL WE SAY ABOUT THE FATHER?

What shall we say about the things that are exalted?
It is fitting that we begin with the Father,
    the root of the Totality,
    the one from whom we have received the grace
    to speak about him.

He existed before anything other than himself came into being.
The Father is unique, the single one, like a number,
    the first one, the one who is only himself.
Yet he is not like a solitary individual who could be a "father,"
    for whenever there is a "father," the name "son" follows.
The single one, who alone is the Father
    is like a root with tree, branches and fruit.
He is unbegotten: no other begot him, nor did another create him.

He is without beginning and without end,
    unattainable in his greatness, inscrutable in his wisdom,
    incomprehensible in his power, infallible in his sweetness.
Whoever has anything is indebted to him because he gives it,
    yet he himself is unwearied by that which he gives.

"The Tripartite Tractate," *NHL*, p. 60-1

WHEN AS NEWBORN INFANTS WE awakened in the morning, our first taste of consciousness was from the breast of our mother, from whom we had so recently been separated. Our primal unity with our mother had been broken by the cataclysm of birth. Our sense of being totally at one with her was forever shattered. Our mother, in whom our whole existence was contained, was present to us as children much of the time, but not always. When she was not there, we sought her, longed for her, hungered for her. Then other people came into our lives—father, brothers and sisters, caretakers, and more. Gradually the child in us came to know that it is but one of many, a small member of a numberless throng.

When the soul in us awakens, it, too, becomes conscious of its separation from the One, unique and single, whom it calls "Father" because it does not know the name of the nameless. He is Father in the sense that he is the source of the soul's life, the planter of the seed of self-knowledge that may germinate in the soul. It is clear that this Father is not a father in the worldly sense for a worldly father is also a son, and this Father is not. Unbegotten, he does not beget; uncreated, he does not create. The Father represents our unattainable awareness of infinity, for there is no place from which he came, nor is there any place where he is not present. There is a paradox here, for the Father is everywhere, yet we do not know him. All living beings, tree, branches and fruit, are parts of the Totality but he is the root that draws up the water of life from the unfathomable depths. This water comes to us as a gift and is therefore to be cherished and the giver adored, for what he gives freely is that upon which we subsist and from which we gain our strength.

But strength for what? Toward what sort of existence shall we direct our lives, in the light of our great indebtedness?

HE ALONE KNOWS

There is no primordial form
    which he uses as a model as he works.
There is no material
    from which he creates what he creates.
Nor is there any substance
    from which he begets what he begets.
There is no co-worker working with him;
    to say anything that suggests otherwise is ignorant.

He is utterly unknowable, inconceivable by any thought,
    invisible to any eye, untouchable by any hand
He alone knows himself, being in himself the Totality.
He transcends all wisdom, and is above all intellect,
    and is above all glory, and is above all beauty,
    and all sweetness and all greatness,
    and any depth and any height.

"The Tripartite Tractate," *NHL*, pp. 61–2

TO HAVE GNOSIS MEANS TO BE able to recognize through the inner eye what is inconceivable to the intellect. Those who have gnosis perceive something that others do not— that the Father cannot be described in the languages of human thought or the patterns of worldly experience. We must come to this knowledge in our own way, through the sensibility of the heart. For this reason, gnostics say that one cannot teach another what the Father is like, but can only say what he is not; thus all their descriptions are negative. This very negativity denies what is an essential tenet of faith in the orthodox priestly traditions: that certain individuals have been designated by divine authority as the only ones who have direct access to "truth," and that those individuals have the right—even the duty—to communicate this "truth" to others.

It may be that this gift is extended to everyone, at least as a potential to be cultivated and refined by contemplation and prayer. Or perhaps, as the gnostics suggest, there are only a few individuals in any given era upon whom is bestowed the wisdom to discern what is true and what is false. Since we cannot know the intention of the Father, we find ourselves asking: "What?" and "From whence?" and we are driven back by the question, "Yes, but what is behind that?" until we are forced to a psychological projection or a philosophical deductive primal cause.

When our minds are full of other people's concepts, views, belief systems or prejudices, it is clearly impossible to incorporate—in the sense of gnosis—anything about the nature of the divine. The human intellect collects thought upon thought and precept upon precept and thinks it knows something; but, when our perception has been emptied and cleared, we realize how little we know. This in itself is great knowledge! It releases us to imagine a time that always was, a time before creation, a time when nothing existed, a time devoid of substance yet charged with an active Presence. When we ourselves feel this empty, when we have let go of all preconceptions and expectations, we become receptive to that active Presence. Our openness creates a space wherein any spark of the divine that glows within us can be fanned by the breath of Spirit. In this way, the utterly transcendent enters into consciousness, and consciousness itself enters into an awareness of the All.

MARKERS ON THE PATH

The Father gave root impulses to all the worlds;
> these serve as markers on the path which leads toward him.
To those who turn toward him, he extends faith,
> and prayer to the Father whom they do not see;
> and a firm hope in him of whom they do not conceive;
> and a love which looks toward that which they do not see;
> and an acceptable understanding of the eternal mind;
> and a blessing, which is richness and freedom;
> and wisdom to those who turn their thoughts
> toward the glory of the Father.

"The Tripartite Tractate," *NHL*, p. 70

THERE ARE THINGS WE KNOW without ever having been told or taught, without ever having seen them or heard them. The newborn infant cries without ever having heard a cry, it nurses without ever having pressed its mouth against a nipple and sucked. The nature of "root impulses" is that they are present without being asked for, since one does not know what to ask for. They are planted in us like roots in the ground, and like roots they reach out in all directions, growing in complexity and acquiring the ability to absorb the richness exuded by the moist earth. These impulses belong to the aspects of us that know without learning, because of the knowledge that is implanted within every human bring and indeed, within every living thing. The flower does not see its roots which nourish it, and we do not see the source of our strength unless we turn toward it, that is, toward the Father.

This prayer is an "annunciation" for us, inviting our consent to enter into a living relationship with the One who has neither beginning nor end. It is a frightening challenge, for we have no moorings of our own in the alien world into which the Father beckons us. The illusory pleasures of the visible world have the substance of sticks and stones; and we believe we can build something out of them. They seem permanent, but in time they crumble and what seemed sure becomes uncertain, what seemed honorable discloses deceit, the clear blue of the sky is obscured by fumes rising from the highways, cool green forests are chopped up into newspaper, and the stories in the newspapers prove to be only propaganda.

If we are not afraid to face the truth, we must see that the visible world is dangerously flawed. The powers of darkness all too often have their way, and they welcome any cohorts who will be seduced into working with them. They tempt us to profit from the corruption that we see about us. The invitation to turn toward the Father is something like this. Embroiled in the immediacy of worldly conflicts, what we see before us overwhelms us. But when we turn toward the Father whom we do not see, we begin to understand our lives from the expanse of infinity. Everything below assumes a different proportion. We see that both the victors and the vanquished soon pass away, and that mountains and valleys are not separate but continuous variations in the contour of the land. Nor are the deepest valleys or the highest peaks extraneous to our own beings. They exist as dual aspects of ourselves and yet as one.

THE FORM OF THE FORMLESS

When the Father stretched himself out for begetting
    and for imparting knowledge of himself to the Totalities,
    he who arose from Him was the first, the Man of the Father.
He is called the form of the formless, the body of the bodiless,
    the face of the invisible, the word of the unutterable,
    the mind of the inconceivable,
    the fountain which flowed from him,
    the root of those who are planted,
    and the god of those who exist.
He is called the light of those whom he illumines,
    the love of those whom he loves,
    the wisdom of those whom he made wise,
    and the power of those to whom he gives power.
He is called the revelation of the things which are sought after,
    the eye of those who see,
    the breath of those who breathe,
    the life of those who live,
    and the unity of those who are mixed with the Totalities.

"The Tripartite Tractate," *NHL*, pp. 67–8.

THE ANCIENTS WHO FIRST CONCEIVED the total other-
ness of an alien God who surpassed all the tribal gods they
knew, wondered what they were to that highest God and how
they might come to know him. He was seen as utterly remote—
not in terms of distance, for gods are usually imagined at a
distance from humanity—but in a place that is more mysterious
than mere distance: a place that is no place, that is beyond all

the worlds we see or can ever hope to see. To reach this God or to be reached by him, it was necessary to bridge the worlds. As they saw it, this was agreeable to the divine intent, for why would all power and all wisdom exist only to be forever imprisoned in an ineffable womb of nothingness?

That human beings exist was sufficient knowledge to lead to the conclusion that the All intended this to be so, and further, that the All wished to communicate in some way to the many. That the many exist was sufficient evidence that the One, the unique and single, wished the many to come into existence. This is the meaning of "when he stretched himself out for begetting." The many then asked of one another, for what purpose does the Father determine that we exist? And those among them who were the wisest, being possessed of gnosis, saw that the One desired to let himself be known by the Totalities, that is, by the many.

As an architect makes a plan before a building is constructed, so it seemed to the wise ones among the many that the one whom they called "the Man of the Father" existed as a plan or archetype in whom the ideal form of humankind was embodied. In order that he might impart the knowledge of his nature to the human race, it was necessary that the Man be given qualities, because the character of ordinary human vision is that it cannot imagine that which is without any qualities whatsoever. What form, then, could be given to the archetype, the model of "the one who arose from the Father?"

In deep humility, the wise ones perceived, or thought they perceived, the intent of the One to represent himself in the being of light who was called the Man of the Father. They saw that the Man's qualities are the *means* through which the unattainable can be reached by human beings and the invisible can be seen. This is what is meant by the "form of the formless, the

body of the bodiless," and all the rest. The Man of light represents the unbounded luminosity of the Father, offered to us. We
perceive it as that wholeness in which we are able personally to
experience a sense of union with the One.

THE FIRST ADAM REVEALED

A voice came forth from the exalted heavenly realm:
   "The Man exists and the son of Man."
And the chief archon, Yaldabaoth, heard it
   and thought that the voice had come from his mother.
He did not know from whence it came.
And the holy and perfect Mother–Father,
   the complete Foreknowledge,
   the image of the invisible one who is the Father of all,
   showed him the first Man.
He revealed his likeness in a human form.

"The Apocryphon of John," *NHL*, p. 111

YALDABAOTH, BEING IGNORANT OF the Father, does not see the light when it first appears. He is, after all, "Samael, the blind god," as his mother called him. But he hears the voice of the one whom the Father has sent in answer to the Mother's prayer for redemption. He realizes that a power greater than his own has descended from the realm of the Father to release the Mother from her entrapment in the domain of the archons.

The first Man teaches Yaldabaoth and the other archons about the holy and perfect Mother–Father through whom everything came into being. When he reveals his image to them in a human form they tremble, and the very foundation of the abyss is shaken. The underside of the waters which were above matter is illuminated by his image which the Man reveals. All the authorities and the chief archon look up, and through the light they see the reflected form of the image in the water.

Like Yaldabaoth, who sees only the reflected light and

believes that he is its source, when we see with our human intellect alone we claim for our own solely that portion of the divine which is revealed to us through the veils upon veils which separate the human experience from the divine intent. But our ancestors, Jew, Christian and Moslem, found other images of the Man of the Father in the mystical traditions of their faith. These same images reside in our own depths, long hidden, longing to be remembered. The Man of the Father stands for the mystical Christ who lives from eternity to eternity, rather than the historical Jesus who lived and taught and died on the cross in a certain time and place. John writes, in the New Testament Gospel that bears his name, of the Man as the emanation of the highest God, who came as a messenger and entered into the man who stood before John to be baptized: "I saw the Spirit descending from heaven like a dove, and it abode upon him."

The Kabbalah, the mystical tradition of Judaism, teaches that the "Man of the Father" is the original emanation of light from the nameless One, called the "En Sof." The emanation took shape as the image of one called Adam Kadmon, a "Man" of light. From his ears, mouth and nose streamed forth lights that produced hidden configurations, so secret that they have never been described until this day. From the eyes of Adam Kadmon poured out the radiant splendor which was to form a central part in creation. The vessels that had been prepared to contain that glorious light broke under its power, shattering the light into millions of particles. These fell into the darkest parts of the created world. There the sparks remain hidden to this day, some in the souls of human beings.

If only we can feel their presence as holy and redeeming sparks in the secret regions of our own souls! Then the Man of the Father will be able to transcend the barriers between earth and the realm beyond the cosmos. Then he will be able to bring to us words and signs from the One who wishes to be known.

THE SECOND ADAM LIVES

Yaldabaoth spoke to the authorities which attend him:
"Come, let us create a man
    according to the image of God and according to our likeness,
    that his image may become a light for us.
The demons and angels worked feverishly
    until they had constructed a natural body.
Their product was completely inactive and motionless
    for there was no spirit in it.
The mother wanted to retrieve the power she had given Yaldabaoth.
She petitioned the Mother–Father of the All, who is merciful,
    to send a holy decree to the angels of the chief archon.
The angels advised Yaldabaoth,
    "Blow into the face of the man the breath of your spirit,
    and his body will arise."
He blew the spirit which is the power of the mother
    into the man's face; but he did not know this,
    for he exists in ignorance.
Yet the power of the mother went out of Yaldabaoth
    into the natural body they had fashioned.
The body moved and gained strength, and it was luminous.

"The Apocryphon of John," *NHL*, pp. 113-16

THE FIRST MAN, OR "THE FIRST ADAM" as some have called him, had disclosed to Yaldabaoth that there is indeed another God, and that the Man was formed in his image. Being filled with envy, the furious archon determined that he, too, should create a man, but in his own likeness. Promptly he set out with his angels and demons to fashion such a creature based on the model of the archetypal Man of light. They worked feverishly to produce their godling, but they worked only with their hands, and they produced a "second Adam" made up only of inert matter. Yaldabaoth had forgotten that he still possessed some of the power of the mother because he was born of her thought which was from the Spirit.

But the Sophia knew, and she wished to retrieve her power from Yaldabaoth and give it to the man he had created, the second Adam, that he might rule over the lower spheres instead of the monstrous archon. When Yaldabaoth blew his breath into the face of the man, he did not know that the spirit was in him. He blew and the body was filled with life and it arose from its stuporous condition. But alas, the powers of the world saw that he was luminous, unlike themselves. They knew in their hearts that he was superior to them and, lest he should rule over them, they took him by force and hurled him into the depths of the abyss. The first Adam, the Man of light, had ascended to the heights to live again as one with the Father. Now the second Adam, the man of intelligence, was overcome by the powers of the world. And as yet no human being had been created.

The makers of this myth must have looked about them and, seeing an imperfect world peopled by imperfect beings, wondered how this might have come to pass. From their own experience as creative people they knew with a sure inner knowledge that whenever one sets out to create, the object which is finally created never equals in splendor and beauty the image that one had in mind. There may have to be one or two or many attempts before anything even remotely acceptable is produced. Why, they must have thought, should it be different with the gods?

Like the mythmakers, all of us live in a world subject to "archons" which cannot abide knowing that there are other powers who are wiser or more beautiful or more generous than they. Often we find ourselves caught in a struggle with these worldly powers which cannot rest until they seduce or banish the carriers of the spirit. Always we face the choice: with which powers shall we align ourselves, and where shall we find our strength?

THE THIRD ADAM GAINS INSIGHT

The beneficent and merciful one, the Mother–Father
    had mercy on the power of the mother
    which the chief archon had brought forth by his breath,
    lest the archons gain dominion over the natural body.
Through his great mercy the Spirit sent a helper to Adam,
    the luminous Epinoia[11], who is the insight of Sophia.
She, who is also called Life, assists the whole creature
    by toiling with him and restoring him to his fullness
    and by teaching him about the descent of his seed
    and also by teaching him about the way of ascent.
The luminous Epinoia was hidden in Adam
    in order that the archons might not know her,
    but that the Epinoia might correct
    the deficiency of her Mother.

"The Apocryphon of John, *NHL,*" p. 116

ONCE MORE ADAM IS RENEWED BY the creator-god and his archons. They fashion him in their own likeness, in the hope that he will come to love his likeness and so willingly serve those whom he resembles. Sophia Zoe, the Wisdom of Life, seeing what they are doing, laughs at their resolve, saying: "Blind are they in ignorance; they have formed him to their own detriment, and they know not what they have done." As descendants of this earthly Adam, we suffer from being controlled by the powers of this world. We are restored to wholeness through insight, the luminous Epinoia of the myth, who lets us know who we truly are, where we came from, and where we are ultimately going. Though we are of a material nature, yet we are also Spirit-endowed, having descended from the realm of Spirit. Hidden within us, as men and as women, is the insight of the Feminine, often called the soul, for we are made both of earth and of the light which the luminous daughter of Sophia has placed within us.

The Gnostics saw the First, Second and Third Adams as prototypes for three kinds of human beings. Yet it is possible to imagine that the secret meaning of this is that these three aspects exist in each person; in some, realized, in others waiting to be discovered.

The First Adam is the model for the *pneumatic* type, in whom the breath of Spirit rules. To the extent that we partake of the pneumatic, our deepest values are concerned with the Father and his realm. Although we live and work in the world of form, we feel alien to it and regard eternity as the true home. This does not mean that we withdraw altogether from the visible world but we are, rather, "in the world but not of it." We do the world's work, but not from a perspective centered on immediate and pressing issues. Instead of focussing on the fragmentary aspects of the world, we see the pieces in the context of an overriding unity.

The Second Adam is the archetypal model for the *psychic* type, in which the psyche, or the inner being, is of greatest moment. To the degree that we see life from the viewpoint of the psychic type, we are aware of our relationship to the divine, yet we have nevertheless taken up residence in this world and deal with it on its own terms. We want to understand the world of nature; we seek also to know its meaning and purpose. Mind and soul are the twin aspects of psyche. Through mind, the realm of the intellect, we try to explain and control the way the world works. Through soul, our intent is to liberate the divine spark that we sense within us.

The Third Adam is the model for the *hylic* type of individual. The word comes from the Greek *hyle*, meaning matter, recalling the Gnostic idea that the first human beings were fashioned by the demiurge out of the earth itself. In our hylic aspect, we are concerned primarily with material things and sensible ideas. As "realists" we are most comfortable with what "is proven" to be true.

Recognizing these three in ourselves and living them fully, allows us to be whole and complete and, therefore, holy.

ΕARLY MORNING MEDITATIONS

Hear me in gentleness, and learn of me in roughness,
I am she who cries out,
   and I am cast forth upon the face of the earth.
I prepare the bread and my mind within.

"Thunder: Perfect Mind," *NHL*, pp. 301–2

ℱIRST THOUGHTS—PRIME

THE ETERNAL FEMININE IS AMBIVALENT from her beginnings. As is characteristic of any archetype—whatever one may say of it, the opposite is also true. Thus she is an aspect of the highest God, and yet she is an entity in her own right. The highest God does not speak for himself, but only through his manifestations and his likenesses. The Feminine does speak; she speaks from on high with the formless voice of "thunder," and in her earthly manifestation she speaks as "perfect mind." As we read her words we will understand that what the Gnostics meant by "perfect" was not an ideal or an ultimate good. A better translation of perfect, would be "whole" or "complete," including all possibilities, both positive and negative.

The Feminine speaks from the place of her wholeness in this amazing document. If the God who contains the entire cosmos and all that lies beyond it can say, "There is no place I am not," then the Wisdom figure can say, "There is no one who I am not." She speaks for woman, whose full role in spiritual life and in the world is not generally recognized, and she speaks as well for the inner impulses in both men and women that are characterized by the many and paradoxical ways she describes herself here.

"Thunder: Perfect Mind" appears to be neither a Christian nor a Jewish writing, for the image of a bold and audacious feminine voice which accepts all the roles assigned to her and even may have initiated them herself would be anathema to true believers of the Judaeo-Christian tradition. Her proclamation would seem perfectly appropriate, however, to people who were used to calling upon such potent goddesses as Asherah, the chief goddess of the Canaanite pantheon, or her daughters Astarte and Anath, or Qadesh, the Egyptian Queen of Heaven. The gnostic Sophia figure reminds us of the active power of the feminine principle as she relates to the masculine powers, and also as she stands alone in her role as "complete mind." As Pronoia, she is the dynamic agent who activates both men and women through consciousness, for it is through her First Thought that divine consciousness escapes the heavenly realms and falls to earth, for better or for worse. Yet she is more than Mind; she is also the one who prepares the bread. She knows, and she nurtures; she leads with her wisdom, and she supports with her compassion. Carrying all this, she becomes heroine, victim, and again heroine, continually shifting her role as she descends in order to assist others in ascending.

As the Sophia, the embodiment of wisdom, she possesses her own identity in the celestial realms, yet she is not content to remain there. When she looks down upon the creation of the visible world and sees that it is flawed, she desires to bring consciousness to that world in order that it might know itself and renew itself. She sends down her intuition (Epinoia) in the form of her own likeness to dwell in the woman who lies beside the first man, that she may awaken him. She comes to him, a rough man of the earth, so that he may learn of her "in roughness," and that he may hear her "in gentleness." But Adam, the man in the Garden, is still ignorant; unaware of the power that is in his mate. Therefore the Epinoia must withdraw from him and from the worldly powers who control him, until he has eaten of the fruit of the Tree of Knowledge, that is of gnosis. Only then can he know what Sophia-Wisdom has revealed to him—the great God's intent in bringing him into existence. Only when he has been enlightened can the true marriage take place and his son Seth, the divine child, be born before Adam dies.

Seth is the prototype of the Redeemer, but he is only the first among those redeeming figures who will follow him. The Redeemer is more than a mystical figure from the tales of antiquity. Redeemers will always come to humanity, as the myth suggests. There are redeemers on earth today. Any of us could possibly be one of them. Redemption happens in ways great and small. Perhaps the small ways are the more important because day by day we have a chance either to redeem or to be redeemed—and these little redemptions help to keep the balance between the dark and the light. The task of redemption is to liberate the light and allow it to be seen in the visible world.

THE PROCLAMATION OF SOPHIA

I was sent forth from the power
and I have come to you who reflect upon me
and I have been found among those who seek after me.
Look upon me, you who see whom I am,
and you hearers, listen to me.
You who are waiting for me, take me to yourselves;
do not banish me from your sight;
Do not speak disrespectfully of me,
nor listen to those who dishonor me.
Do not be ignorant of me anywhere, or at any time.
Be on your guard!
Do not ignore me!

"Thunder: Perfect Mind," *NHL*, p. 297

IN OUR MEDITATION, LET US RETRACE our steps to a time about two hundred years after the death of Jesus. We stand in the marketplace of Alexandria, where people from Europe, Africa and Asia move around—philosophers and saints, beggars and prostitutes. In this colorful cosmopolitan city where the cacophony of sounds is accompanied by smells of incense and dung and fresh meat and the garbage floating down the river, small crowds gather here and there around street preachers and teachers who sell their philosophies as others sell bread and love philters. Stop to listen to those new Christians who are attracting more people day by day. They speak of a god-man, sent down as a messenger from his heavenly abode to let the world know about the glories of the father. Is he any different, we wonder, from the Jewish prophets who spoke of their god as an all-powerful father and king, creator of the world, absolute ruler and judge? Something important is missing here. We hear no mention of the mother-god, the goddess who appears in a thousand guises, she about whom we have heard in the tales of the Egyptians, Greeks, Romans and Babylonians.

The goddess has not yet been totally banished by the Jewish-Christians; they simply do not speak of her. They are devoted to one called Mary, who gave birth to the son of the Most High. She was a mortal woman who served as a vessel to receive the divine impulse. In her own right she is no more or less than any young Jewish virgin betrothed to an ordinary man. She becomes an object of veneration only because the Most High has chosen her.

But the goddess—*there* is a female with real presence! She speaks for herself and knows who she is. In this moment she is not at ease, for the converts to the new faith have forgotten her warnings. They follow in the footsteps of their Jewish forebears who banished her altars from their cities in Palestine. So we walk on, hoping to find a place in Alexandria where she is still remembered, and there among the Egyptians and Greeks and the others whom the members of the new sect call "pagan," her voice rings out in the marketplace.

Hers is a strong voice, the voice of independent femininity and creative maternity. She speaks for the defenders of the older faiths. Crowds of people stop to listen, for they have seen how unyielding is the power of the male god when it is not tempered by the goddess's passionate love for humanity and divinity alike. They adore the foolish mercy she bestows upon all without discrimination when she stretches out her arms to the multitudes. Through the mouths of those who still honor her, she proclaims her strength and demands the respect due to one who was the First Thought of the Father. And so we stop to listen to those who would tell us about the role of the Feminine in creation and in the redemption of those who have gone astray.

THE AMBIVALENCE OF THE SOUL

I am the first and the last.
I am the honored one and the scorned one.
I am the whore and the holy one.
I am the wife and the virgin.
I am the mother of the daughter.
I am the members of my mother.
I am the barren one and many are my sons.
I am she whose wedding is great, and I have not taken a husband.
I am the slave of him who prepared me.
I am the ruler of my offspring,
    but he is the one who begot me before time was,
    and he is my offspring in due time,
    and my power is from him.
For I am knowledge and ignorance.
I am shame and boldness.
I am strength and I am fear.
I am the one who is disgraced and the great one.
Give heed to me!

"Thunder: Perfect Mind," *NHL*, pp. 297–8

THE FEMININE IS TO THE MASCULINE as the Soul is to the Mind. Each is an aspect of the whole; the one without the other is incomplete. As long as Mind and Soul, Masculine and Feminine, are locked in an endless embrace, the whole exists but it is static. When the Feminine declares herself as "I," Soul takes her place beside Mind and she begins to function in her own way, which is different from his way.

She speaks first of her timelessness: "I am the first and the last." In this way she declares her coexistence with the Highest God who has neither beginning nor end. She was with him always, and will be with him forever. Because she has separated herself from the Father in whom she was enclosed, she can now assume a duality of her own. Her qualities express the most profound paradox of her existence, being one with the Father yet being one in herself. She differs from the Father in that he is spoken of only in terms that glorify and exalt him, while she declares herself in terms of polar opposites: "I am the honored one and the scorned one." Being the consort of the Father, she is honored, but having dared to think for herself without his consent, she brings scorn upon herself. When she is at rest in the heaven beyond the planets and the fixed stars, she is the holy one; when she descends to the lower realms out of love for those below, her all-embracing love earns her the epithet of "whore." She fulfills the abundant roles of the Feminine: mother of the daughter, the one and single, and the mother of many children. She is subservient to the All, yet she rules over him, or overrules him, when she uses the power that comes from him to follow resolutely her own path of mercy and compassion.

Paradoxical as is her nature, the eternal Feminine knows who she is and demands that we pay attention to her. Doing so, we recognize in her the reflection of our own soul, which is feminine in nature whether we are physically male or female. While our minds remain aloof and impartial as they observe what is before us and judge it accordingly, our souls rejoice with those who rejoice, and suffer with those who suffer.

The soul's feeling for all creation draws us into the midst of relationships, and she cannot rest until we have set them aright. If our intellects insist on our being in the right, our souls can see the validity of both sides of any question. Mind is the part of us that always seeks to be in charge, to win every struggle; while soul wants to negotiate where there is conflict and help to bring about a resolution that is agreeable to all sides. Soul recognizes its ignorance as well as its knowledge, its fears as well as its strength. Soul also serves as an intermediary between the visible world and the invisible world.

THE SPEECH THAT
CANNOT BE GRASPED

Hear me, you that hear
    and listen to my words, you who know me.
I am the hearing that can be acquired everywhere,
    and I am the speech that cannot be grasped.
I am the name of the sound
    and the sound of the name.
For what is inside of you is what is outside of you,
    and the one who fashioned you on the outside
    is the one who shaped the inside of you.
And what you see outside of you, you see inside of you;
    it is visible and it is your garment.

"Thunder: Perfect Mind," *NHL*, p. 302

THE WORDS OF THE SOUL EMERGE from a mystery and they are a mystery. They suggest to us that the outer life and the inner life are reflections of one another. Neither has an independent existence, although they seem to, but the separation of the world within from the world without is an illusion. How subtle is the wisdom in her words, "I am the hearing that can be acquired everywhere; I am the speech that cannot be grasped!" It is one thing to perceive the sound of the words but quite another to understand what they mean for our own existence and how they demand that we behave. Hearing is something that we can do without much effort, but grasping the import of what we hear requires us to open ourselves to all that is present in our lives with neither expectation nor prejudice.

The wisdom of the soul tells us that we cannot separate ourselves from what is outside of us, since everything that we see is shaped by what we are. As we bring our essence into confrontation with the visible world, we color it with the colors of our own being. Whatever we see before us is affected by what we bring to it. If we are angry, we see others through the lens of our anger; if we are deceitful, we regard others with suspicion; if we are trusting and compassionate, others will speak freely to us.

Name and sound, sound and name—how are they different? One is the perception and the other validates it. Yet there would not be a name without the sound of the name. And if it is kept secret, if it is not pronounced, the name and the sound still remain in a state of potentiality waiting to be expressed. So, when the soul speaks to us in silence, we ought to listen and hold her wisdom in silence also, until the moment when it seems right to give it voice.

The soul tells us that the one who has made the inner world has also made the world without, and that what is outside of us is also inside. This is a statement of the essential unity of all that exists, an assertion that we are made of the same stuff as are the stars and that our movements are not isolated from theirs but rather part of an all-inclusive process. If we listen to the words of the living soul within us, we will know that we move with the rhythms of the universe. We are truly separate, in the sense that every note in a symphony is separate from the others, but we are also one with the All, with the many sounds of earth and sky that blend together to produce harmony or discord.

THE TREE OF GNOSIS

The revelation to John continues:

"The archons took Adam and placed him in paradise,
    and they said to him, 'Eat, that is, at leisure.'
For their luxury is deceptive and their beauty is depraved,
    their trees are godlessness, and their fruit is poisonous,
    and their promise is death.
They placed the tree of their life in the midst of paradise.
The root of this tree is bitter and its branches are deadly,
    its shadow is hate and deception is in its leaves;
    and its blossom is the ointment of evil,
    and desire is its seed, and it sprouts in darkness.
The plan they made together is like their spirit.
But what they call the Tree of Knowledge of good and evil,
    is of the Epinoia of the light.
They stood in front of it that Adam might not look up at it
    and recognize his nakedness."
I, John, asked, "Lord, did not the serpent teach them to eat?"
The savior smiled and said, "It was I who caused them to eat."

"The Apocryphon of John," *NHL*, pp. 116–17

THE GNOSTICS THOUGHT OF Paradise as a vale of sensual pleasures fashioned by the archons to deceive humanity and lead it into self-indulgence and forgetfulness. The Garden is filled with the seductions they devised to keep its inhabitants in ignorance and submission. The Tree of Life that they placed in the Garden is the tree of *their* life, and its fruits are material things contrived to lull people into ease and complacency. This tree sprouts in darkness and can only take root and grow where there is no insight and where it is easy to forget that human beings are intended to be, above all, carriers of consciousness. In such a place we tend to reach only for what appears to be within easy grasp, without thinking of the consequences. The self-serving uses of sexuality and power may satisfy immediate desires, but all too soon other temptations appear and new desires seize possession of individuals and of nations.

The other tree in the Garden, the one the archons attempt to conceal from the primal couple, is the Tree of the Knowledge of good and evil, or the Tree of Gnosis. The archons did not make this tree: it is from the realm of light, and the Epinoia of the light is in it. The authorities hide it from Adam, fearing that no authority can stand in the face of knowledge of the truth. The Epinoia, being the insight of the Sophia, is kin to the spark of light hidden within Adam, but he does not yet know that this is in him. He only knows that the authorities have declared what he shall and shall not do, and he dreads their power.

Here is the model for those who are content to live by blind faith, without questioning what they are told as long as it comes from 'a respectable source.' They are unaware that the breath of the Sophia moves in each of us, enabling us to distinguish the counterfeit spirit that exists on earth from the true Spirit that cannot be contained in any place but exists everywhere.

We might think this is all a sinister plot on the part of the archons and the authorities to rule the world in accordance with their own design. But the messenger lets John know that what has occurred is according to the will of the Father, since nothing happens but by his will. This follows from the teaching that the divine plan or cosmic order is incomprehensible through the intellect, but that nevertheless we can observe its workings if we will look about us with eyes that penetrate below the surface. The serpent taught the primal couple to eat of the Tree of Knowledge so that they might learn of begetting and lust and destruction, and thus be useful to him.[12] But that they were allowed to listen to the serpent and turn away from the path of light, is also ascribed to the will of the Father, for it is our human fate to have within us seeds of darkness as well as seeds of light.

THE LIGHT HIDDEN IN EVE

Because the Epinoia of the light had hidden herself in Adam,
    the chief archon wanted to bring her out of his rib.
But the Epinoia of the light cannot be grasped.
Although darkness pursued her, he did not catch her.
And he brought a part of his power out of Adam,
        and made of it another creature in the form of a woman
        according to the likeness of the Epinoia.
He brought the part which he had taken from the power of Adam
        into the female creature, and Adam saw the woman beside him.
In that moment the luminous Epinoia appeared.
She lifted the veil which lay over his mind,
        and he became sober from the drunkenness of darkness.
He recognized his counter-image and said,
        'This is indeed bone of my bone and flesh of my flesh.'
Therefore the man will leave his father and his mother
        and cleave to his wife, and they will be one flesh,
        for the eternal ones will send him his consort.
When the Sophia came down in innocence to rectify her deficiency
        through her Adam and Eve tasted the perfect Knowledge,
        and they were awakened in their thinking.

"The Apocryphon of John," *NHL*, pp. 117–18

THE OPPOSITES ARE CONTAINED IN THE first man, and all who come after him. Adam is formed of the red earth,[13] while the light from beyond the sky is embodied in the luminous Epinoia. Adam is the offspring of the conjunction of opposites, having been conceived after the initial separation of the All into its masculine and feminine aspects. The archons are envious of Adam because of the spark concealed within him; the spark they wish to grasp and keep for their own. But in their ignorance they do not know that the divine cannot be taken by force, and so the earthly powers fail when they try to take possession of the spiritual powers. Out of the envy which is the essence of their nature, they then attempt to fashion their own creature, taking for its substance a part of the power of Adam, but not, as the biblical tradition says, his rib.

What can be the meaning of "the power of Adam"? When we consider that the archons wished to make slaves of the human race, the power which enslaves a man especially with regard to women can only be his semen. If this is the substance from which the archons created Eve, it is clear enough that they meant to keep the human race under their control by seeing to it that it become obsessed with sexuality. So they bring forth Eve, whom they model after the Epinoia; but she is only a likeness, and not the spiritual woman. Yet Adam looks upon her with wonder. The Epinoia sees this and appears to Adam. Shedding her light upon him, she dispels the darkness of his ignorance. When he has acquired insight, Adam recognizes her. She enters into his counter-image as his soul, and imparts to him the knowledge of the Spirit from which she came. Now man and his soul are one, male and female, complete in themselves. Adam and Eve can leave the innocence of their childhood and his dependence upon their earthly parents for, as mature individuals, they will establish their own relationship with heaven and earth and with each other.

From this beginning, the gnostic tradition regards male and female as absolutely equal, with each requiring the other for its completion. Wholeness, a precondition for holiness, demands that the two aspects of the individual act in accord with one another. Though physically we are male or female, spiritually we are androgynous, partaking in both feminine and masculine energies. In our earthly existence this ideal is not so simply achieved. The spark of "insight" threatens any part of us that is vulnerable to the worldly powers. To be awakened means to recognize that beauty is not beauty which hides suffering and casts a veil over injustice, but that beauty is found when can see the light of Spirit shining in all beings and all things.

EVE BETRAYED

Yaldabaoth clothed Adam and Eve in darkness
    and cast them out of paradise.
He saw that the virgin who stood by Adam was luminous,
    for the Epinoia of life was in her,
    and he desired to seduce her.
But the Foreknowledge of the All looked down and saw
    and she snatched the Epinoia of life out of Eve.
The chief archon, ignorant of this, seduced the woman's likeness,
    and begot in her two sons, Eloim and Yave.
Eloim has a bear face and Yave has a cat face.
Eloim is unrighteous, but Yave is righteous.
Yave he set over fire and wind, and Eloim, over water and earth.
He gave them principalities, that they might rule over the tomb,
    and he called them Cain and Abel with a view to deceive.
Sexual intercourse continues to this day due to the chief archon
    who planted sexual desire in her who belongs to Adam.
He produced through intercourse the copies of the bodies
    and he inspired them with his counterfeit spirit.

"The Apocryphon of John," *NHL*, pp.117–18

WHEN THE PRIMAL PAIR HAVE eaten of the Tree of Knowledge and received gnosis, the creator-god who made them both sees that the virgin Eve is filled with light. He envies her beauty and innocence and desires her for himself. He cares nothing for her person but wants only to inseminate her, so that his offspring and not Adam's shall rule the world. The only "father" Eve has ever known casts his incestuous net of seduction about her. But the ever-watchful Sophia, knowing beforehand what is coming, once again outwits the chief archon. Through her magical devices, she splits Eve's personality in two. The soul or essence (Epinoia) separates herself from the physical likeness (Eve) and withdraws up into the Tree of Knowledge. Only her cast-off shell, the earthly garment, is defiled and fouled by the archon, while her true self looks on from a distance, maintaining her purity by hiding her real nature.

The myth is relived today whenever an innocent child or trusting adult is abused or raped. Whether the damage is physical or emotional or both, the demon of Power has overcome the child of Love. No wonder that the psyche splits in two. What is defiled is the inert material body, while the part that is spirit-endowed flees into the Tree of Knowledge. By disengaging ourselves from the horrors of our lives, one part of us manages to escape from a reality that is too terrifying to bear, while the other endures it without the slightest feeling. Later, when the soul returns to the body, we may forget the whole episode. Yet once we have been a victim of an unspeakable crime we will never be quite the same afterwards, for we will have lost our innocence. When sexuality awakens in a person who has been betrayed, it may be a sexuality divorced from love which only goes through the motions of relatedness, while the true self is disconnected from its core. The person feels alienated from something, but does not know from what.

What is the fate of the offspring of an unholy union who arise not from the Spirit, but from a counterfeit spirit? The names "Eloim" and "Yave" have a familiar ring, like the names of old Semitic tribal gods that were worshipped before the Hebrews became a cohesive people under the protection of the deity who revealed himself to Moses on Mount Sinai. The ruler of darkness gives to his two sons the right to subdue the four elements of nature—fire, wind, water and earth—out of which he had created the world. His sons "Cain" and "Abel" are also the split-off parts of Yaldabaoth; Cain is the victimizer, and Abel, the victim. Neither of these beings is whole or complete. How could he be, with a heritage of envy on the one side, and subterfuge on the other? Nor can any of us be complete unless we recognize the opposites within us and come to terms with them.

SETH THE REDEEMER

I

When Adam recognized the likeness of his own foreknowledge,
    he begot the likeness of the son of Man.
He called him Seth, according to the way of the earthly race.

"The Apocryphon of John," *NHL*, pp. 119

II

In his seven hundredth year Adam said to his son Seth,
    "Listen to my words:
"When God created me out of earth along with Eve, your mother,
    I went about with her in a glory
    from the world from which we had come forth.
She taught me the word of knowledge of the eternal God
    and we resembled great angels,
    for we were higher than the gods who had created us.
Then the God who is ruler of these worlds separated us;
    the glory fled from us, and knowledge of the eternal realm,
    but it entered into the seed of the great realm.
Since that time we learned about dead things, like men.
We recognized the God who had created us, and served him,
    and darkness came upon our eyes."

"The Apocalypse of Adam," *NHL*, p. 279

I

SETH IS THE SON CONCEIVED AFTER Adam and Eve have awakened to gnosis.

II

Adam reveals to Seth the secret of his birth, how three great angels shining in glory appeared to him and to Eve so that they knew that these were not servants of the god who had created them. "They said to me, 'Arise, Adam, from the sleep of death, and hear about the realms and the seed of that man to whom life has come, who came from you and from Eve, your wife.' When we heard these words from the angels, Eve and I sighed in our hearts. The god who had created us heard, and he said to us, 'Why were your sighing in your hearts? Do you not know that I am the god who created you? And I breathed into you a spirit of life as a living soul.' Then darkness came upon our eyes and the vigor of our knowledge was destroyed in us and weakness pursued us. The days of our life became few, and I knew that I had come under the authority of death." Then Adam tells his son what the angels have revealed to him, that it is his destiny to carry the light that was shut up in darkness (in nature and chaos) up to the higher light in the form of understanding, in order that the separation between matter and soul may be healed and human nature may thus be made whole.

This act of redemption has been brought about only partially, since the powers of the natural world still strive against human aspiration, and struggle to retain part of the light for themselves. Humanity's battle for the liberation of light against the powers of darkness is the subject of the Gnostics' radical revision of the biblical myth. Seth is regarded as the ancestor of the incorruptible race, the pneumatics, who devote themselves to the quest for inner wisdom. In our own day, there are those who take upon themselves the Sethian task of bringing light to those who are willing to see. They soon learn that the darkness does not remain inactive. With the aid of an opposing "counterfeit spirit," the archons still try to lead human beings away from the true path. The demiurge brings Destiny into the picture as a means to bind the gods, angels, demons and human beings with instruments of measurement and time and the seasons as fetters, that he may hold all of us in his power. When this is not effective, he sends catastrophes, like the great flood in biblical times, but even these do not work, for hope remains and Noah is delivered.

Adam tells Seth, and through him all human beings, that even when the darkness is most profound, a Redeemer will surely come, one who will perform signs and wonders that will heap scorn upon the powers of darkness and their rulers.

MID-MORNING
MEDITATIONS

The gospel of truth is joy for those who have received
from the Father of Truth the grace of knowing him ...

Since oblivion came into existence because the Father
was not known, then if the Father comes to be known,
oblivion will not exist from that moment on.

"The Gospel of Truth," *NHL*, p. 40

FIRST THOUGHTS—TERCE

"THE GOSPEL OF TRUTH" IS AN UNTITLED book which takes its name from the first line. Truth and knowing how to find and recognize it is the subject of the book and, in a wider sense, it is the major theme of all of the Gnostic writings. It is essential to understand how the Gnostics sought truth, if we are to appreciate why gnostic ideology was excluded from the basic body of orthodox doctrine when the Christian bible was canonized. Orthodoxy establishes institutional structures for the Church—bishops, priests, canons and rituals. These then become ultimate authorities, authorities that are external to the personal experience of the individual.

The very existence of such a document as "The Gospel of Truth," makes it easy to see why the Early Church hierarchy decried Gnosticism as "heretical." Even in a time when the Church was still divided into many communities and sects, authority was invariably placed in some sort of hierarchy. Gnostics were contrarians who trusted personal revelation and sought direct knowledge of the order of the universe. At the same time that they recognized that they could not understand the divine intention through any effort of intellect, they saw themselves as expressions of that divine intent and therefore as carriers of the divine purpose and meaning in the visible world.

They believed that the only way to come to know the other-worldly God whom they called "Father" was to know themselves, since they themselves were expressions or manifestations of the Father. They could not accept the authority of a hierarchical structure that would stand between them and the divine word, to interpret it for them.

In the Gnostic view, it is given that in our youth we are all ignorant of our presence as a part of the divine Unity, and unaware that this divine Unity is also within us. The human experiences that precede the acquisition of gnosis are ordeals of anguish and terror. There is much in the world that is strange and threatening to us. Often we do not know how to move about without being overwhelmed by powers that are beyond our ability to control or manage. Insecurity and fear dominate human consciousness. This fear is directed both outside of ourselves toward aspects of our lives over which we have little ability to exercise command or, alternatively, it is turned inward as we perceive our weaknesses and limitations. But the objects of our fears are not real; they are only perceptions based upon our lack of self-knowledge. As long as we see ourselves as frail creatures confronted by a hostile world, or as losing our balance in the face of superior forces, we are in fact surrendering our natural power. We are alienated from our source of support, and we do not even know that such a source exists.

Nevertheless, there is bound to be a messenger. Sometimes the messenger appears as a teacher coming from afar to bring the requisite knowledge, and sometimes as a voice speaking from within. The messenger prepares the way for the soul's liberation from the bondage of ignorance and its ascent to knowledge of the divine, which is within us and yet beyond us. What characterizes the gnostic is an ability to hear the voice of the messenger, and a willingness to attend to the message.

The work of the gnostic is to bring about the redemption of the spark of truth, or light, in the visible world that illumines that which is invisible.

Woven together in "The Gospel of Truth" are strands of wisdom from Athens, Rome, Alexandria and Jerusalem, those teeming centers of religious fervor that birthed the philosophy of the Gnostics. "The Gospel of Truth" is a testament to the God within, who calls to us from the very center of our beings. If this God seems near to us, it is because we hear when we are called. If this God seems distant, it is because we have not discovered that neither space nor time can separate us from the mystery to which we belong, and which belongs to us.

THE ANGUISH OF IGNORANCE

When the totality asked, "From whom have we come forth?"
    ignorance of the Father brought about anguish and terror.
The anguish grew solid like a fog;
    no one was able to see that the totality was inside of him,
    the Father, the incomprehensible one
    who is superior to every thought.
For this reason error became powerful,
    working on its own matter foolishly, not knowing the truth.
It set about a creation, preparing it with power and beauty,
    as the substitute for the truth.
As for the incomprehensible Father, who made the totality
    the totality is within him and the totality needs him.
Although he did not give perfection to the totality
    but retained it within himself,
    the Father was not jealous.
Indeed, what jealousy indeed could there be
    between himself and his members?

"The Gospel of Truth," *NHL*, p. 40

IN BLINDNESS AND IGNORANCE, THE human race wanders about in search of its origin and its destiny. People seek these outside of themselves, as though human consciousness could discover itself in something alien and distant. Knowing ourselves to be imperfect individuals living in an imperfect world is the beginning of wisdom. Imperfection implies its opposite: perfection must exist, if only as an ideal toward which we strive. When we attempt to find truth outside of ourselves and fail to confirm it through our personal experience, we become prey to ideas and practices that serve the purposes of those who devise them.

Declining to trust our inner resources, symbolized as the interior "Father," we become vulnerable to the fads and fancies of the hour. We get caught up in the need "to have" and lose sight of the need "to be." The need to have "works upon its own matter." Having begets only a greater need to have, as our desires increase with every new acquisition. To accumulate material goods requires the cultivation of the power to possess, which translates into purchasing power. Soon mere goods are not enough, and the concept of "beauty" comes to be associated with the goods we obtain. The more powerful we are, the more beautiful our possessions must be. Or so we believe. This does not mean that there is something wrong with the appreciation of beauty, or with surrounding ourselves with beauty. It is only when beauty becomes the sign by which we can recognize the power of the one who holds it, that it turns into a sham.

A woman has been stricken with cancer. She has undergone surgery and radiation and chemotherapy, yet despite remissions the cancer has broken through again. During her illness she has deepened in her understanding of the will of the Father and has accepted it. She has served as an example of steadfastness, cheerfulness and courage on every step of her painful journey. As she enters the terminal phase of her illness an unearthly beauty surrounds her. Shining from her eyes is a luminosity one rarely sees in this world. Her face is relaxed and calm, unlined despite her mature years. Soon she will lose everything she possesses in this life, and it is clear that she is clinging to none of it. Having is no longer important to her, if indeed it had ever been. Being is all, and she is being that for which she was put upon this earth.

What is truth but making space in our lives where insight may enter?

IF YOU ARE CALLED

Those whose names he knew in advance were called at the end.
One whose name the Father has uttered has knowledge,
    and one whose name has not been spoken is ignorant.
Indeed, how is one to hear if one's name has not been called?
One who is ignorant until the end is a creature of oblivion,
    and will vanish along with it.
Therefore, if you have knowledge, you are from above.
If you are called, you hear, you answer,
    and turn to him who is calling you, and ascend to him.
And you know in what manner you are called.
Having knowledge, you do the will of the one who called you,
    you wish to be pleasing to him,
    you receive rest.
Each one's name comes to him, and you who hear your name called
    know where you come from and where you are going,
    as the drunkard who has turned away from his drunkenness,
    and having returned to himself, has set himself aright.

"The Gospel of Truth," *NHL*, p. 42

SOME PEOPLE ARE ENDOWED FROM their birth with the capacity to acquire "the wisdom of the heart." Those who have this knowledge have been identified by the Father, and they will be called by name, that is, specifically and individually. These persons hear when they are called, they pay attention, and they move in the direction of the One who calls. They appreciate the importance of having been called and so they do what is asked of them.

It may seem elitist to some to say that only certain people are destined for the gift of gnosis, but on a deeper level it is not. The possibility of being called may exist in any one of us. How, then, are we to know whether we are called to receive the knowledge of the heart? As with all gifts of grace or understanding, we only know that they are ours in the moment when we perceive that they have been given to us. "The call" is such a gift; it is the still small voice within us that lets us know what is of significance and what is not, what is true and what is false. It does not speak of socially acceptable values or consensual truths, but rather of the integrity of individuals both within themselves and in their relationships with others.

Knowing one's name means that one is the same person in every relationship and in every situation. One does not veer away from one's sense of self for the sake of expediency or to gain favor from someone. Even if we are born with the capacity to be fully ourselves, we often lose sight of it. Gnosis comes through attention to the inner life, and this demands that we curb our obsessions with material possessions and sensual pleasures. Like strong drink, these may be acceptable in moderation, but when they become primary goals, they result in forgetfulness. As long as we sleep the sleep of oblivion, we will not be likely to hear when we are called. Asleep, we cannot know whether or not we are destined for gnosis. Awake, we may hear ourselves called to attention by the voice that reminds us: "No place is empty of Me."

ONLY PARTS ARE REVEALED

The Father reveals his bosom, which is the Holy Spirit.
He reveals what is hidden of him, which is his son;
 so that through the mercies of the Father
 the realms may know him
 and cease laboring in search of him,
 but rest in him, knowing that this is true repose.

"The Gospel of Truth," *NHL*, p. 43

THE UNKNOWN GOD OF THE Gnostics cannot be revealed as a totality to those who seek him because each of us is a part of that totality, and a part cannot grasp the whole. For this reason only parts or aspects of the Father are revealed to us. If we conceive of God as one body, then the revelation of his bosom is a revelation of that aspect which is closest to the heart, the feminine wisdom that is sometimes called the Holy Spirit. From this bosom also comes forth the Son, who is born of the union of the Father and the Holy Spirit. The Son is sent out into the world (the aeons) in the form of a man to bring the word, or logos. Being of the same substance as the Father, the Son represents the Father in a way that human beings can relate to personally, so that those who recognize the Son need no longer search about in darkness for the unknown Father. This recognition brings rest.

Herein lies the mystery of Unity and plurality or, put another way, the paradox of wholeness and diversity. Most of the time we see our world in bits and pieces, individuals and groups, nations and continents, planets and solar systems. Even when we think in terms of systems theory, where everything is a part of a larger system and contains within it a smaller system, we must finally ask, what is the sum of it all? This is the mystery we cannot name, for to name it would be to say what it is and therefore to imply what it is not. But if we, and everything we see and imagine, are parts of something greater that is contained in the All, is it not to be expected that we should yearn for the totality from which we feel split off?

If we understand ourselves to be portions of Unity or, in theological terms, "children of God," then we, like divinity, exist on two levels: one, which begins to take form at conception, and the other, which enters into that form but is not contained by it. A portion of eternal life enters into the womb when the ovum accepts the sperm, and with the exhalation of our last breath it departs to return to the totality.

If only we could see, when threatened with destruction, that the eternal part of us can never be destroyed, we would not cling to life when it ceased to have meaning, nor would we fear death. We would regard birth and death not as beginnings or as endings, but as events that bracket a brief passage of time on an endless journey. As we look back through the ages to a time when the Neanderthals roamed about, or to the classical eras of Greece and Rome, or to the invasions of the Huns and Vandals, or to the Crusades, it is easy to see that these were just such brief events in time that came and went. One part of us wisely asks: Will it be any different with us? The aspect of ourselves that knows from where we have come, knows also where we are going.

THE DISSOLUTION OF FORM

When he has filled the deficiency
    the Father will abolish the form; that is, the world,
    in which the son had served.
The place where there is envy and strife is deficient,
    but the place where there is Unity is perfect.
The deficiency came into being where the Father was not known;
    when he becomes known the deficiency will no longer exist.
As in the case of a person who is ignorant,
    when he comes to knowledge his ignorance vanishes of itself.
As darkness vanishes when light appears,
    so also deficiency vanishes in perfection.
From that moment on, form is not apparent
    but will vanish in the fusion of Unity.
Within Unity, each one will purify himself
    consuming matter within himself like fire,
    darkness by light, and death by eternal life.

"The Gospel of Truth," *NHL*, p. 43

FORM BELONGS TO THE VISIBLE WORLD, which is only a fragment of Unity, therefore deficient in comparison with the fullness of the invisible world. As the ideal precedes the real in Plato, as formlessness precedes form in Zen, as the collective unconscious precedes individual consciousness in Jung, so in gnosis, Unity (the Father) precedes the fragmentary world. The term "deficiency" as applied to the fragmentary visible world in which we live, is not necessarily pejorative; it merely implies lack, or limitation. What is lacking is the special kind of knowledge called gnosis. In contrast to the way the practical arts and sciences are concerned with factual and specific knowledge of the forms in this world, gnosis looks to the universal context in which all forms exist.

This is beautifully expressed in the ritual of a contemporary gnostic church where, just preceding the mystery of the eucharist, the priest recites the following: "Hear the words of the immortal Logos: 'Gather all my limbs which, since the foundation of the world, have been scattered abroad in this aeon, and reunite them together and receive them into the light!'" And when the mystery is complete and the rite is ended, the following is added: "I have recognized myself and gathered myself together from all sides. I have gathered together my limbs that were scattered abroad and I know thee who thou art." [14]

The words perfection, unity, wholeness and fullness, all share the same meaning. They serve as ideals toward which we may aspire, even with our limited consciousness. It is not required of us that we eliminate our "shadows," those darker aspects of our being that we often fail to recognize or refrain from acknowledging. On the contrary, unless we recognize our own ignorance and errors, we cannot attempt to correct them. When we have not identified the darkness in ourselves, we tend to project it onto others and say, "your error," not "my error," and "your ignorance" not "my ignorance." Perhaps it is no mere happenstance that so many individuals have achieved moral leadership in our world only after having spent long years in prison or isolated by illness—people who had the will and took the occasion to look deeply within themselves and differentiate their own private issues from the issues of others and to clarify what was truly of value to them and what was error. In the process, material things lost their overweening importance for these people, but the unceasing search for wider consciousness provided the fire that warmed their hearts and enlightened their minds.

WHOM SHALL WE SUPPORT?

Speak of the truth with those who search for it,
    and of knowledge to those who have committed sin in error.
Make firm the foot of those who have stumbled
    and stretch out your hand to those who are ill.
Feed those who are hungry, give repose to the weary,
    raise up those who wish to rise and awaken those who sleep.
If strength acts thus, it is even stronger.

Be concerned also with yourselves;
    do not be concerned with things you have rejected.
Do not return to what you have vomited, to eat it.
Do not be moths. Do not be worms; you have already cast it off.
Do not become a dwelling place for the devil,
    for you have already destroyed him.
Do not strengthen those who are obstacles for you,
    who are collapsing as though you were a support for them.
The lawless is someone to treat ill, rather than the just one.
So you, do the work of the Father, for you are from him.

"The Gospel of Truth," *NHL*, p. 47

WHEN WE SPEAK FROM THE WISDOM of the heart, that is, from gnosis, our words are illumined by the light that streams from the invisible world of the Father. When words come to us in this manner, they speak the truth and offer knowledge to those who wish to correct their errors. But speech alone is insufficient; we are obliged to act on behalf of those who do not know what we may know. In enacting what we understand, we become stronger. Being concerned about oneself keeps one from being caught in the destructive behavior of others. Doing all this helps us to fulfil the purpose for which we have been given life.

There are three questions that we are likely to ask ourselves when we have become aware that we possess the knowledge of the heart. The first is: To whom may we speak of it? The second is: How shall we act upon it? And the third is: How shall we avoid being drawn into the traps and snares that beset our path? In answer to the first question, we are told to speak our own truth to people who truly desire to hear us and whose fault or error is not knowing who they are or whence they have come. Such people live in darkness as though they were blind—they stumble, they falter. By supporting them and nurturing them, we bring light to them. In answer to the second question, we are told to help those who express a desire to become more conscious, yet not to neglect to activate the possibility of inner development in those who are as yet oblivious to it.

The answer to the third question recognizes the importance of taking care of ourselves because, as we work toward increasing our consciousness and that of others, the only tool we have is our own subtle awareness. To preserve our integrity, we need to discriminate between that which strengthens us and that which hinders us. It is not wrong to reject negative influences in our lives, but when we do this we often fall into the danger of becoming remorseful and losing our resolve. This is what is meant when we are warned not to eat that which we have vomited. We are not to become moths that fly about senselessly after everything that appears attractive. Nor are we to become worms, chewing on what is over and done with. Nor are we to support those whose addictions or neuroses only become stronger as we make allowances for them or refuse to confront them, for they will drag us down with them.

People without inner discipline work only for themselves, while those who reflect upon their actions work for others as well as for themselves. Cultivating this inner discipline, we may become bearers of the light, and the light will shine through us.

WATER, ICE, AND FRAGRANCE

The Father is sweet and in his will is what is good.
He recognizes his children by the fruits of their works.
The children of the Father are his fragrance;
    he loves his fragrance and manifests it in every place.
He causes it to surpass every form and every sound,
    for it is not the ears that smell the fragrance,
    but the breath, that attracts the fragrance to itself
    and is submerged in the fragrance of the Father.
Thus he shelters it and takes it to the place where it came from,
    from the first fragrance which is grown cold.
It assumes a psychic form, like cold water which has frozen.
While it is not truly solid, those who see it think it is earth,
    yet afterwards it dissolves again.
If a breath draws it, it gets hot;
    for the fragrances that are cold are from division.
Faith comes to dissolve the division in the warm pleroma of love
    so that the cold may not return,
    but in its place, the unity of perfect thought.

"The Gospel of Truth," *NHL*, p. 47

ALTHOUGH THE FATHER IS UNKNOWN, his manifestations are like a fragrance, ineffable yet sweet. This
fragrance is not manifested throughout the visible world as
form, but intangibly, as light and as the breath. Though the fragrance is not solid, yet it appears to be "real" in the concrete
sense, just as ice appears to be solid but dissolves quickly when
it is warmed. When water turns to ice it acquires the semblance

of separate solid blocks, but when it is warmed it flows together as water; when it is still warmer, it evaporates into the air as fragrance. One does not come to know the fragrance through hearsay but through one's own experience, breathing it in and being inspired by it. Faith in this process brings about a love that is felt as the pervading force which generates life to fill the emptiness (the pleroma). Such love brings together and unites the temporal and the eternal.

How then can human beings relate to an invisible Author of chaos and cosmos? The use of the word "fragrance" suggests that he is not to be thought of as male (or female, for that matter) but as an incorporeal substance. This beautiful metaphor expresses the subtlety and the penetrating quality of the relationship that can exist for those who have faith that such a relationship is possible. Formless in itself, the fragrance enters into every form. It holds the power to attract us to the spiritual element in our lives. We are told that our own breath draws forth this fragrance. Through the very act of consciously breathing in and out, we participate in the mystery by which the essence of the divine and the essence of the personal intermingle continuously, each partaking of the other.

When this occurs, we are no longer isolated individuals subject to all the sadnesses of separation: feelings of abandonment, isolation, loneliness, rejection and inadequacy. Rather, we recognize that we are intimately involved in a single unity composed of a totality which would be incomplete without sentient human beings, just as a fragrance cannot become known unless there is someone to breathe it in.

POSSESSING NO THING,
LACKING NOTHING

This is the manner of those who possess
  something of the immeasurable greatness from above
  as they wait for the One alone and the perfect One,
  the One who is there for them.
They do not go down to Hades
  nor have they envy nor groaning nor death within them,
  but they rest in him who is at rest,
  not striving nor being twisted around the truth.
They themselves are the truth; and the Father is within them
  and they are in the Father, being perfect,
  being undivided in the truly good one.
Being in no way deficient in anything,
  they are set at rest, refreshed in the Spirit.

"The Gospel of Truth," *NHL*, p. 51

THOSE WHO HAVE UNDERSTOOD and acted upon their knowledge of the magnitude of the invisible world live consecrated lives as they wait for their ultimate return to eternity. They do not allow the darkness of ignorance to encompass them, but find peace through knowing who they are, where they have come from, and where they are going. Because of their joy in what they know, they envy no one; nor do they fear pain, for pain is transitory; nor do they fear death, for death is a release from the world of limitations and an opening into eternity. They rest secure in the knowledge that they will find peace; so why should they exhaust themselves with striving or with rationalizing to get around the truth? They realize their place in the totality, and they realize the place of the totality in themselves. They lack nothing, for they are filled with Spirit.

Here is the culmination of "The Gospel of Truth." It speaks of the manner of life of the one who has been called, who hears the call, and who responds to it affirmatively, accepting all that this entails. What is willingly offered up corresponds to the evangelical virtues of monasticism, which are all about not possessing. Poverty, chastity and obedience translate into: you cannot possess any *thing*, you cannot possess any *person*, and you cannot possess *time*. *The Rule of St Benedict* says that you are to do the thing as soon as possible, as thoroughly as possible, and restore your tools when you are finished. The thing must be done with vigor and without murmuring.

The phrase "They are set at rest," may have to do with anxiety. We are called to do a thing and we may do it. But we wonder if we really were called, if we really know how to do it, and if we really ought to do it. As these questions crowd in before the doing, our anxiety increases. Many of us are called, but few choose to answer, for answering means to let go of our attachments to fragments of reality and to the values that characterize a fragmented world view, as we try to see the Whole and our small part in its workings.

If we are to live in peace in the visible world, we had better accept this world as it is and do all we can to cultivate harmony in our small part of it. The key to negotiating the delicate balance between the worlds is to appreciate what is desirable in the mundane world without becoming trapped in our desires or attached to our possessions, our image, our status, or our ambition.

The vital question is, where is our primary commitment? This question assails us when we find that what society approves does not necessarily accord with the way we are called to live. "Answering when we are called" often means sacrificing the approval and support of the group, to go our own way. We may have to reject the group norms and at times we may even reject consensual reality, the wisdom of the head, in favor of gnosis, the wisdom of the heart. The way of the Father appears hard, but for those who can say yes to it, the way is clear, coherent and without conflict. This is what is meant by saying, "They do not go down into Hades."

MIDDAY MEDITATIONS

Whoever has ears, let [them] hear.
There is light within [men and women]
   of light, and [they] light up the whole world.
If [they] do not shine, [they] are in darkness.

"The Gospel of Thomas," (24), *NHL*, p. 129

ƑIRST THOUGHTS—SEXT

THE FINDING OF INNER WISDOM, called "gnosis," through self-knowledge is the theme of "The Gospel of Thomas,"[15] from which all the texts for Sext are drawn. Another expression for inner wisdom is "The Kingdom of the Father." Just as with all gnostic language, the "Father" is not to be taken literally as a description of someone or something that only exists apart from humanity; rather it is an expression of something we experience in our inner lives. The Father within represents the essence of the individual that flows into the single cell of origin with the convergence of genetic streams at the moment of conception. More properly, this source of wisdom could be called "The Kingdom of the Father and the Mother," for these Parents-within engendered every person alive today, as it was with all who preceded us. The Kingdom of the Father and, implicitly, of the Mother, contains the wisdom born out of the collective experience of humanity, which is renewed in every generation. We experience this old wisdom today as distilled and concentrated in the consciousness of individual human beings. Here wisdom reposes. Here it is to be sought. Here and only here will it be found.

Our social environment, with its goals of getting and spending, imposes obstructions between ourselves and the attainment of wisdom, or gnosis, and we ourselves suffer from our incomplete perceptions of what surrounds us. We need a guide to lead us through the labyrinth of appearances—one who has already transcended many of the conflicts in which we ourselves become absorbed and which separate us from the Kingdom. In "The Gospel of Thomas", the sayings of Jesus are offered as a guide to the invisible world of spirit for those who recognize that the visible world is not the only reality. Here "Jesus" stands as the one who is able to manifest in words that wisdom which goes beyond words. If we are to attempt to understand the sayings attributed to Jesus, we will need to look beyond the words to the hidden meanings toward which they point.

"The Gospel of Thomas" begins: "These are the secret sayings which the living Jesus spoke and which Didymus Judas Thomas wrote down." It is through introspection that we discover our eternal companion, or "twin."[16] In the Syrian gnostic tradition, Thomas, the privileged disciple, was thought to be the brother of Jesus. Thomas recognizes Jesus, perhaps not as a literal "brother," but as an eternal twin or counterpart who is not only in the world but also in himself. We need to remember, of course, that this is mythology, and not history. Gnostics have been accused of "mythologizing" history by bringing about a division of the Christian redeemer into two completely separate beings: the earthly and transitory Jesus of Nazareth, and the heavenly and eternal Christ. We have seen similar dualities in the paired figures of the alien God and the demi-urge, the prototype of the Second Adam and the Adam of the Garden, and the Sophia/Epinoia and Eve. It was clearly not the intention of the Gnostics to present history in their writings, but rather to tell their "secrets" in the symbolic language of the soul that, in our own time, we call mythology. The myth is not true in any literal sense, yet it arises from a profound wellspring, the truth of the psyche inspired by Spirit.

We cannot understand mythology by using the ordinary terminology commonly used in the visible world, for mythic language applies to the timeless world where there are no boundaries; hence the saying that introduces "The Gospel of Thomas:" "Whoever finds the interpretation of these sayings will not experience death." We may understand this to mean that whoever discovers the meaning in these sayings will not experience life or death in the ways that are dictated by conventional wisdom. If we come to understand these words we may discover, as did Didymus Judas Thomas, that Jesus is our "twin," our spiritual "other self."

Jung describes the personal self as that central axis in each of us upon which our total being rotates, both conscious and unconscious; and the greater Self as the central aspect of the All, the "Father," upon which the axis of the universe revolves, including all its visible (conscious) aspects as well as its invisible (unconscious) aspects. This greater Self, or Father, makes itself known through the individual self. Unless we know ourselves, we cannot know the Father. Nor can we find the "Kingdom of the Father" unless we look within ourselves. "The Gospel of Thomas" may be seen in Jungian terms as the book of the Self. The figure of Jesus, the one who urges the seeker to discover his own identity as a carrier of the spark of light, may surely be understood, as Jung suggested, as a symbol of the Self.

FINDING THE KINGDOM WITHIN

Let him who seeks go on seeking until he finds.
When he finds he will become troubled.
When he becomes troubled, he will be astonished
    and he will reign over all.

"The Gospel of Thomas" (2), *NHL*, p. 126

If those who lead you say to you:
    'See, the Kingdom is in the sky,'
    then the birds of the sky will precede you.
If they say to you, "It is in the sea,"
    then the fish will precede you.
Rather, the Kingdom is inside of you, and it is outside of you.
When you come to know yourselves, you will become known
    and you will realize that it is you
    who are the sons of the living Father.
But if you will not know yourselves,
    you dwell in poverty
    and it is you who are that poverty.

"The Gospel of Thomas," (3), *NHL*, p. 126

AN INTERPRETATION THAT ARISES from the inner recesses of the heart often strikes us with sudden awareness. It troubles us to recognize that it was always there before us, but that because of our ignorance or blindness we did not see it. Self discovery invariably involves inner turmoil. How

difficult it is to look into the darkness and listen in silence! It is
far easier to seek out those who have ready answers for us, saying, "It is in the sky," or "it is in the sea."

The world abounds with people who are ready to advise
us and who eagerly tell us what they think we need to hear.
Their attitude of sureness and their willingness to give pat
answers come from their being conversant mainly with the
material world where answers are possible if one is given either
the requisite facts or a ready-made belief system. They look to
objective data, to rational solutions, to anything outside of
themselves for proofs—since they see themselves as separate
individuals who are detached from the objects of their search.
They do not recognize that much of what troubles individuals
has little to do with objective reality but more with the mystery
of their own experience which is embedded in every thought
and every act, making it something more, or something less,
than it seems to be to the casual observer.

The "living Jesus" who speaks his wisdom is not the one
who died on the cross, but one who descended to this plane
from the level of reality that we call the invisible world and
whose essence returned to the invisible world when he departed
from his earthly form. His words reveal to us that the Kingdom
of Eternity is within us, as it is within him, and it is within all
human beings. As seekers, we may be astonished when we find
that the Kingdom to which we aspire is so close at hand! In the
intimacy of our quiet meditation we come to know our own
darkness and, when we have penetrated it, we may find there the
hidden fragment of the boundless Light that is the treasure of
the Kingdom within.

To know ourselves is to acquire consciousness of both
the limited and the unlimited aspects of our beings. This
knowledge of the heart is not available to those who have not

personally engaged themselves in the search for the Kingdom. Such people dwell in spiritual poverty, and they themselves are that poverty.

LIVING YOUR TRUTH

That which you have within you will save you
    if you bring it forth from yourself.
That which you do not have within you will kill you,
    if you do not have it within you.

"The Gospel of Thomas," (70), *NHL*, p. 134

IT SERVES NO PURPOSE TO CONCEAL who we are or what we know. Knowing ourselves and being willing to stand for who we are makes life authentic. If we can do this, then we can move freely through life because there is no dissonance between our sense of our own nature and the way we behave. But whoever is unable or unwilling to do this stores up poisons that eventually destroy the integrity of the person.

That is the dark secret which we carry. Because we have not brought it forth it lies heavy within us, weighing us down. We grow accustomed to it, and days pass with our scarcely being aware of it. Yet it is always present, awaiting an incident to stir it up—usually something that would appear insignificant to anyone else—but for us it acts like a magnet that draws our energy to it so that we feel depotentiated. As time goes on we become ever more defenseless because we ourselves cannot let go of that which holds us in its grip.

Why do we cling to that which burns in us like a slow fire, gradually desiccating us, and yet we are not consumed? Perhaps it is because we have condemned ourselves to a shame that we dare not expose. Is there no one before whom we can appear naked in our soul? No one who would understand without judging? What human being can transcend moral judgment?

"That which you do not have within you, will kill you if you do not have it within you." What is the it? Can it be that very judge whom we seek outside of ourselves and despair of finding? Can it be the one who knows the darkness, the dark god, the god of the underworld? It has been said that the Kingdom of Heaven is within. Can it be that the Kingdom of Hell is within also? If the bright god, the creator and ruler of the universe and a thousand suns, is within us—is not the dark god, the denizen of chaos, the destroyer of love and of relationship and of young soldiers and of helpless animals and of the air we breathe and of sanity—is not that god within us also?

If we project these gods outside of ourselves, and say that they are beyond us and too great for us to comprehend, then surely they will destroy us. But if we learn to know them as aspects of ourselves, and knowing them accept them, they will not kill us but will save us. For true knowledge (gnosis) lies in this awareness: that all that you see outside of yourself is also within, and whatever you discover within yourself, that also is in the world.

BODY, SOUL AND SPIRIT

Woe to the flesh that depends upon the soul;
    woe to the soul that depends upon the flesh.

"The Gospel of Thomas," (112), *NHL*, p.138

If the flesh came into being because of the spirit,
    it is a wonder.
But if the spirit came into being because of the body,
    it is a wonder of wonders.
Indeed, I am amazed at how this great wealth
    has made its home in this poverty.

"The Gospel of Thomas," (29), *NHL*, p.130

THE GNOSTICS OF ANTIQUITY SAW the visible world as separated from the invisible by a veil of sky, black as midnight. As they gazed into the darkness they imagined that the stars were tiny holes, pinpricks in the veil through which intimations of the light beyond could be glimpsed. If the separation between the worlds was intensely real and painful for them, their yearning to penetrate the mystery was equally real. We come to know the worlds through the soul, or psyche, the carrier of consciousness. She inclines her face in one way or another, either toward the world of the body and all material things, or toward the Spirit and the mysteries of the invisible world.

Of the twin paradoxes: "Woe to the flesh that depends on the soul," and "Woe to the soul that depends on the flesh," the first suggests that the flesh, the body, and the material world cannot be anything but what they are, matter dealing with the condition of matter in a material world. In this world we need to function as pragmatists, resolving the issues that bind us fast and refusing to allow the darker powers, the archons, to take possession of us. If we obsessively fix our eyes upon the soul, we can easily overlook things that need attention in the material world. With these out of sight, we exist in ignorance and we depend on the soul to rescue us somehow from the results of our blindness.

The soul is equally vulnerable when she depends upon the material world to justify her existence. When she attempts to bring more consciousness to human beings, she finds to her dismay that most of us want only to be rescued from some specific uncomfortable condition. Her purpose, however, is not to solve problems in the material world, or even to intercede with the Father for those who call upon her when they are in distress. Her desire is not for the world in itself, but for the holy sparks of the divine that are encapsulated in ignorance. She yearns to liberate them so that they can be seen for what they are, immortal aspects of our own beings that know why we have been put here and for what purpose we exist. Yet she must keep a respectful distance from the concerns of the body and materiality, lest she once more fall under the power of the archons, who make their home in the house of our own ignorance.

If the flesh came into being as a tangible expression of the Spirit, it is clear that our task is to lend ourselves, body and soul, to the Spirit, for the work of disseminating the light through whatever means are given to us. A world devoid of Spirit is surely a dead world. The counterfeit spirit of the archons prevails throughout much of the created world in false gods, false values and vain desires. To know this and to be able to live in this world without being corrupted by it is not easy. Yet gnosis teaches that it is possible to shed the layers of ignorance like worn-out garments.

DISCERNING WHAT IS
BEFORE YOUR EYES

I

They said to him:

"Tell us who you are that we may believe in you."

He replied:

"You read the face of the sky and of the earth,

drawing your own conclusions,

but you do not recognize the one who stands before you,

and you do not know how to read this moment."

"The Gospel of Thomas," (91), *NHL*, p. 136

II

A woman from the crowd said to him:

"Blessed are the womb which bore you and the breasts
which nourished you."

He said to her:

"Blessed are those who have heard the word of the Father
and have truly kept it,

for there will be days when you will say,

'Blessed are the womb which has not conceived
and the breasts which have not given milk.'"

"The Gospel of Thomas," (79), *NHL*, p. 135

I

WE READ IN MATTHEW 16:2-4, that when the Pharisees and the Sadducees came to test Jesus they asked him for a sign from heaven. He answered them, "When it is evening, you say, 'It will be fair weather, for the sky is red.' And in the morning, 'It will be stormy today, for the sky is red and threatening.' You know how to interpret the appearance of the sky, but you cannot interpret the signs of the times." Like them, many people today are all too ready to accept the voice of temporal authorities about matters that are not easily understood. They want the secrets of the mysteries to be revealed to them, and the quicker the better. They are willing to base their conclusions on superficial appearances, but not so ready to explore what lies beneath the surface.

Certain parables from the gnostic Gospel of Thomas contradicted the prevailing position of the Early Church by undermining the exclusivity of the male lines of authority. For the dissenters who composed these texts, true authority resided only with the All, the androgynous Mother–Father whom, for convenience's sake alone, they lovingly called "Father."

The Logos[17] says, "You do not recognize the one who stands before you and you do not know how to read this moment." This can only mean that in a deep inner sense we already know when truth stands open before us, but we fail to recognize it, perhaps because of the strict demands that truth makes upon us. There is no place for expediency when we attend to what is beyond the present moment. To read the moment is to know that it is only a leaf floating on the current of time, moved about by unseen currents and subject to the will of the wind. To read the moment is to sense the timeless matrix in which the temporal event occurs, to see the whole without being distracted by the fragments.

II

The same applies to the feminine principle. Associated over the years with woman and her physical nature, the Feminine has been valued as birthgiver and nurturer. Women have accepted being defined as enablers of men, and tradition has hallowed this role in the visible world. A woman who has not taken this role upon herself is often made to feel less valuable than her more nurturing sisters. The Logos seems to take issue with this idea. Though he does not depreciate the maternal feminine, he acknowledges another source of grace. Whoever has heard the call of the Father and has lived in accordance with it is truly blessed. The Logos makes no distinction here between the masculine and the feminine principles. Both can gain access to the word of the Father, and both can serve in whatever ways they are asked. So she who has "not conceived" or "whose breasts have not given milk," that is, the woman who does not depend upon the male or serve the male but who is one in herself, is as worthy of blessing as the one who enacts the traditional feminine role.

THE ELUSIVE KINGDOM

I

His disciples said to him, "When will the Kingdom come?"
"It will not come by waiting for it.
It will not be a matter of saying, 'Here it is' or 'there it is'
Rather the Kingdom of the Father is spread out upon the earth,
    and you do not see it."

"The Gospel of Thomas," (113), *NHL*, p. 138

II

The Kingdom of the Father is like a certain woman.
She took a little leaven, concealed it in some dough
    and made it into large loaves.
Let him who has ears hear.

"The Gospel of Thomas," (96), *NHL*, p. 136

III

The Kingdom of the Father is like a certain woman
    who was carrying a jar full of meal.
While she was walking on the road, still some distance from home,
    the handle of the jar broke
    and the meal emptied out behind her on the road.
She did not realize it; she noticed no accident.
When she reached her house she set the jar down
    and found it empty.

"The Gospel of Thomas," (97), *NHL*, p. 136

I

IN THE GNOSTIC MYTH, THE KINGDOM is a realm devoid of time and space, where there is neither past nor future. For the past to exist it must already have ended, and for the future to exist there must already be the concept of beginning. The Kingdom of God is the eternal realm that exists in the present and only in the present. When will it come? It is already here: it comes as we come upon it; it moves into our awareness as we become attentive to it. Those who ask the question do not know this. When we truly know this we do not need to ask the question.

II

The loaves of bread appeared to become enlarged by themselves, however this was not due to their efforts but to the small bit of leaven that was hidden in them. But of course the loaves did not know that they had become large. It occurred in oblivion. We come upon what is concealed through what is revealed; therefore the wise teacher speaks in parables. We ourselves may spontaneously undergo a transformation due to the divine spark that is in us, but we are not excused from redeeming the spark from oblivion. This is the meaning of the saying, "Let him who has ears hear." Over and over again, these words summon us to attention.

III

She who does not pay attention to the gifts she possesses labors over them as though they were heavy burdens, but it all comes to nothing. The gifts of the Spirit are proffered generously, but we can easily dissipate them as we go about our business paying little attention to their value. We become distracted from the tasks that have been set for us. Our attention wanders. We neglect to notice when we have compromised the aspirations to which we have committed ourselves. Our spiritual strength departs from us so slowly and quietly that we do not notice it. Perhaps we are even relieved to feel our burdens becoming lighter. But when we come home, that is to the awareness of our true origin and our purpose in this life, it is only then that we find that we have lost the treasure which we so eagerly sought.

WHAT WILL YOU WEAR?

I

Do not be concerned from morning until evening
and from evening until morning
about what you will wear.

"The Gospel of Thomas," (36), *NHL*, p. 130

II

"When will you be revealed to us, and when will we see you?"
"When you disrobe without being ashamed
and take up your garments
and place them under your feet like little children
and tread on them.
Then will you see the son of the living one,
and you will not be afraid."

"The Gospel of Thomas," (37), *NHL*, p. 130

I

WE READ EARLIER, "YALDABAOTH clothed Adam and Eve in darkness and cast them out of paradise." The garment is a symbol of the seductive means used by the archons to tempt us into assenting to their system of control based upon envy and desire. As creatures of the creator-god, the desire to be seen as powerful is implanted within us. Fashions are designed to communicate status and authority; they change rapidly, playing upon the insatiable human desire to be the first, out ahead of the crowd and the one who is looked to for leadership. The garment stands for everything we put on to enhance our self-image and the manner in which we show ourselves to others in the visible world. It is also a possession that we have chosen for ourselves in order to make a personal statement. Self-involved as we become, "concerned from morning until evening," we forget that we are also endowed with seeds of the light that do not need to be covered up, but rather uncovered.

II

The Rule of St Benedict is very clear about those who commit themselves to the spiritual life. The brethren are continually reminded that all things are given for their temporary use and that they pass away or are returned to the one who gave them; therefore one should not be attached to anything that one owns.

In dreams, the clothing that we wear and our relation to it often tells a great deal about the way in which we encounter our world. Jung called these outer trappings the "persona," after the Greek masks that were used in dramas to suggest the character the actor was playing. He said that we all use our personas—and clothing is a part of the persona—to create an impression in the world and to facilitate an easy movement through all types of relationships. We may wear a number of different personas depending upon what the particular situation calls for. As a means of adaptation, the persona is not negative in itself, but it can become dangerous when we identify with it and say, "I am that." We create a false self-image and then we go on to believe that this represents us accurately. We see ourselves as denizens of the visible world, wise to its ways, and we lose sight of the real world that is within us and beyond our understanding.

So the disciples, and we among them, are taught that we will not see the messenger from the invisible world until we can disrobe without being ashamed, and put our garments under our feet and tread on them. We are required to present ourselves authentically in this world, standing unashamed just as we are. If we are willing to strip our self-image down to its essentials, we will see our spiritual essence, and we will not be afraid.

THE MYSTERY AT HAND

I

Seek and you will find.
Yet what you asked me about in former times,
    and which I did not tell you then,
    now I do desire to tell,
    but you do not inquire after it.

"The Gospel of Thomas," (92), *NHL*, p. 136

II

Recognize what is in your sight,
    and that which is hidden from you
    will become plain to you.
For there is nothing hidden
    which will not become manifest.

"The Gospel of Thomas," (5), *NHL*, p. 126

III

Cleave the wood and I am there;
    lift the stone and you will find me there.

"The Gospel of Thomas," (77), *NHL*, p. 135

I

WHEN WE WERE CHILDREN, THE WORLD was a mysterious place. We were not always sure where the line was between fantasy and reality. We moved back and forth easily between the visible and the invisible worlds and did not even see any barriers. We were intensely curious about the nature of things and never tired of asking questions. Then, as we were growing up, we began to hear that the time was not right, that we were too young to understand the answers to our questions. The curtain dropped down, and we waited for the time when we could see again what was happening behind it. Perhaps we grew tired of waiting; perhaps we became engaged in other matters, perhaps we even forgot to inquire after what we once so eagerly sought.

II

When at last the curtain opens and the mystery play is performed, we do not even see it. It is then that the voice which comes from beyond, is also the voice within. It reminds us that attention is the first requisite for receiving gnosis. The place to begin is in the present, and in the visible world.

Who is before us, and what is in range of our vision? The Spirit reveals itself first in human experience—in the trusting eyes of a friend, in the trees that stand between earth and sky purifying the air we breathe. Until we learn to be attentive to the sights and sounds of the phenomenal world, we will not be able to see the grander vistas or hear the celestial music. The eternal is within the temporal, the magnificent in the mundane.

III

Some people fret about their daily tasks and complain that these subvert their attention from contemplation and from appreciation of the works of the one whom we call the Father-Mother. And so the Logos is sent, in the form of the word, and the word is within hearing. It is in everything we say or do, in every person we meet, in our very thoughts. The word itself cannot tell us what something is, much less can it reveal what the nothing is. Yet words can touch the heart, conjuring up images that are familiar, images carved out of wood and stone—the sculptors' media.

This wood and this stone in their natural form only hold meaning for us when we endow them with meaning. Who is it that we find when we cleave the wood and lift the stone? Can it be an inner image of perfection, the spark of holy light that, although hidden within us, yearns to become manifest? If this be so, therein lies the promise—that through the quality of our attention to the visible world, the invisible world may become manifest.

Afternoon Meditations

I descended to the midst of the underworld
and I shone down upon the darkness. It is I
who poured forth the water. It is I who am
hidden within the radiant waters. I am the
one who gradually put forth the All by my
Thought. It is I who am laden with the Voice.
Through me gnosis comes forth.

"The Trimorphic Protennoia," *NHL*, p 513

FIRST THOUGHTS—NONE

THE WRITERS OF THE GNOSTIC BOOK "The Exegesis on the Soul" might well have titled it "The Evolution of the Soul." It is one of those tales of romance and wonder that emerged out of the polycultural scene of Alexandria, probably from the pen of Jewish-Christian[18] cosmopolitans who were familiar with the heroines of Greek novels and myths. The Greeks left their mark most strongly on the culture of gentile Christians, influencing them to idealize the woman of virtue, while regarding the fallen woman with utter disdain. Jewish-Christians differed in their attitudes from the gentile Christians, for the former had the heritage of the Old Testament in their veins, as well as much Jewish apocryphal literature of the centuries immediately preceding and following the time of Jesus.

Jewish Christians wrote of a feminine soul that incorporated all the charm, beauty and grace of the Hellenic lady as well as the dark scheming aspect of the sinful woman of Judaic lore. Among the women of the Bible who acted out the metaphor of the duality of the soul were Ruth, who had manipulated if not seduced Boaz into marrying her; Bathsheba, who was certainly a virtuous woman until King David invited her into his bed; the widow Tamar, who played the prostitute in order to seduce her father-in-law; and Rahab, the only one who was a professional prostitute, and who believed that the God of Israel desired the ancestral land for his people and who saw herself as representing the fertile ground that was to be given to its future inhabitants who would cultivate the Promised Land. Every one of these women, despite the transitory loss of her own personal integrity, was able to see the true light when it appeared to her, to purify herself, and to become whole again.

Scholars have suggested that the gnostic author of "The Exegesis on the Soul" may have been a woman, basing their conjecture on the powerfully evocative feelings expressed that, in their minds, could only have been experienced by a woman. Such intensity wells up from woman's awareness of the sanctity of her own body, and the outrage, shame and humiliation she feels when her body is abused and defiled. The pain is least of all physical; the wound to the soul causes far more suffering. If the soul is, indeed, to be thought of as feminine regardless of one's physical sex, we can readily understand the theme and argument of "The Exegesis of the Soul:" that the feminine is vulnerable because she is pregnable, because she can be entered into and possibly contaminated. The soul is, after all, psyche, and psyche is composed of both mind and emotion. Mind, or intellect, deals with the visible world in a practical way, solving problems, considering issues, and accomplishing what needs to be done to sustain life and to enjoy it. Emotions temper the mind; they come unbidden and exert tremendous power over us, even when we may be unaware of their presence.

If the Logos, which appears in masculine form, represents an expression of the word or the light, then the Sophia, the soul in its feminine form, represents that which receives the word or the light. Her presence is needed for the completion of the divine program for those who live in the world: to find the lost fragments of the Spirit, to know them for what they are and to liberate them, thereby regaining wholeness through them. In this, the soul reaches out to her brother, the Logos.

If soul truly means psyche—that tortured, ambivalent aspect of ourselves that reigns over our thoughts, feelings and behavior—then the characteristics of the soul as set forth in this text are experienced by men as well as by women. Soul is the archetypal vessel that is given form in order to be able to carry the holy seed, but she can fall upon bad times and be defiled. Then she must be purified and renewed before she can be restored to the condition of wholeness, or, as it is called in the sacred myths, the condition of "virginity." The process of the soul's descent into the depths of the unconscious, its awakening into awareness and its emergence into the light of consciousness, is what Jung meant when he spoke of the "individuation process." Though such a process can never be adequately described in words, the metaphor of the soul's journey reveals the agony and the glory that attend the experience.

THE HOLY PROSTITUTE

Wise men of old gave the soul a feminine name.
Indeed, she is female in her nature as well; she even has a womb.
As long as she was alone with the father,
    she was virgin and in form, androgynous.
But when she fell down into a body and came to this life,
    she fell into the hands of many robbers.
The wanton creatures passed her from one to another;
    some took her by force, others seduced her with a gift.
They defiled her and she lost her innocence.
She prostituted herself, giving her body to one and all;
    each one she embraced, she considered to be her husband.
Even when she turned her face from those adulterers,
    she ran toward others.
They compelled her to live with them
    and render service to them upon their beds,
        as if they were her masters.
Out of shame she no longer dared to leave them,
    while they deceived her, pretending to be faithful
        as if they greatly respected her.
After this, they abandoned her, and went away.

"The Exegesis on the Soul," *NHL*, p. 192

I N THE BEGINNING THE ONE WHO is called "Father" was alone, being the All which filled the entire existence. The soul, by her very nature, is a partial being, having come into existence through her separation from the Totality. Before she was, she and the Father were one alone and androgynous: neither was the Father male nor the Sophia female. The myth of the pri-mordial androgyne in the Greek world is as old as Empedocles, and Plato suggests in the *Symposium* that what human beings call love is nothing other than the divided halves of the One longing to be reunited.

The androgynous condition is the ideal for those who would live a life in service of the Spirit, for it cannot be realized in a physical body, but only through the psyche. In the world of flesh, body has form and form is inescapable. "Separating from the Father" means assuming an identity, taking the liberty of having a thought of one's own, and leaving the protection of the abode of silence. The soul descends, or rather falls, to a lower plane where she is trapped in a body. She finds herself caught in an evil world, and the creatures of this world use every possible means to bring disgrace upon her. At times she submits; at times she persuades herself that she must do what she does. How poignantly her frantic efforts to save herself are described! These are not alien to the efforts that many people put forth in the world to evade, avoid, and finally to embrace the alluring and beguiling powers. Those who have become addicted to the pleasures they have so dearly bought for themselves make all sorts of allowances for prostituting the soul. They become dependent upon those who would exploit them and they know it, but they see no way out. They try to get along with the archons of our contemporary world by making concessions to them. At last, having abandoned their personal integrity, they themselves are abandoned by those who have broken their spir-its in the world into which they have fallen.

We hear much today about abused women and molested children, and violated men for that matter. How many of them return to those who have mistreated them, hoping that they will keep their promises, that this time it will be different! Perhaps we, too, are among the suffering. If the grinding pain that is caused by continuing compromise or compliance wears us down so that our lives lose all meaning, it may be time to withdraw and to reflect upon what has happened to ourselves and to the society in which such offenses to human dignity are tolerated.

THE REPENTANT WIDOW

The soul becomes a poor desolate widow, without help;
　　nor is even any food left from the time of her affliction.
From the adulterers she gained nothing except the defilements
　　they gave her while they had sexual intercourse with her
And her offspring by them are dumb, blind, sickly and stupid.

But when the Father who is above looks down upon her
　　and sees her sighing, with her sufferings and disgrace,
　　and repenting of the prostitution in which she engaged
And when she begins to call upon him, that he might help her,
　　crying out with all her heart:
　　"Save me, Father!
　　I will repay you for abandoning my home.
　　Restore me to yourself again!"
When he sees her in such a state, he will have mercy upon her,
　　for many are the afflictions that have come upon her,
　　because she abandoned her home.

"The Exegesis on the Soul," *NHL*, pp. 192–3

IT WAS A VITAL PART OF THE GNOSTICS' view that the divine spark which lives in human beings can be made conscious. Their philosophy is echoed in the apocryphal Wisdom of Solomon: "O Lord, you who love the living, your immmortal spirit is in all things." (12:1) Although some dogmatists deny it, even the Bible puts forth this idea: "Then the Lord God formed man of the dust and breathed into his nostrils the breath of life, and man became a living soul." (Genesis 2:7) Alexandrian Jews identified "the breath of God" with the God-within. They took this passage to mean that the divine spirit sleeps in us, and that through great effort and attention it may be awakened. Integrating some views of the Greeks—Plato, the Orphics and the Stoics, who considered the human soul to be a part of the deity—these cosmopolitans believed that the daimon (or spirit) within us is akin to, and of the same nature as, the God who pervades the All.

Even though the soul, in her dejected state of "widow-hood," does not remember that the spark is within her, yet it is through the glimmering of that spark that she becomes vaguely aware of the other world where the Father abides. She does not know yet that she will be called upon to redeem the spark by bringing it fully into consciousness. In pain and anguish she cries out for help. She repents what she has done and vows to make amends for what she has brought to pass. She begs the Father to restore her to himself and to her place in the original unity. What she asks is not simple; it is the task of a lifetime, perhaps of many lifetimes: to bring together fragments of the eternal light that were scattered abroad in the visible world.

The terrifying state of the lost soul calling out to God in fear and trembling is a precondition for becoming whole again. She realizes, as we all realize at one time or another: I *absolutely* do not know who I am, yet he *absolutely* knows. It is the sunken feeling of wanting with all your heart not to exist at all. Having descended into the darkest depths of the shadow, the soul returns, not so much to experience the mercy of God as to find out who she is *now*. There is a kind of riddle in this text—what is a "virgin prostitute"?—until one applies it to oneself; then it becomes a dreadful question about one's identity. What, for example, is an "ignorant scholar"? What is a "killer surgeon"? What is a "peace-keeping general"?

It is not enough for us to be conscious of the divine presence; it is also necessary that we confront our own selves and our errors due to ignorance. We may be outraged that we must repent of our ignorance, for how could we know we should have known what we did not know? But repent we must. The soul must repudiate her unwholesome involvement with the experiences of her former life before she can embark on her ascent to the Father.

TURNING THE WOMB INWARD

As long as the soul keeps running about everywhere,
  copulating with whomever she meets and defiling herself
  she exists in suffering, and justly so.
But when she perceives the straits she is in
  and weeps before the Father and repents,
  the Father will have mercy upon her.
He will make her womb turn from the external domain
  and will turn it again inward,
  so that the soul will regain her proper character.

When the womb of the soul,
  by the will of the Father, turns itself inward,
It is baptized, and cleansed of the external pollution
  which was pressed upon it,
  like dirty garments which when put into water
  and turned about until their dirt is removed,
  become clean.
In this way, the cleansing of the soul
  is to regain the newness of her former nature,
  and to turn herself back again.

"The Exegesis on the Soul," *NHL*, p. 194

WHEN WE ARE IGNORANT OF HER presence, the soul runs about aimlessly like an orphan child to whom no one pays attention. She explores all sorts of places and, since there is no connection with the inner Self to warn her where danger lurks, she knows neither fear nor caution. She solicits affection from any likely source. Easily deceived by flattery, she goes to whomever offers her the appearance of pleasure; yet she finds no pleasure in intimacy with strangers. Since she does not know where she belongs, she looks everywhere for a place to call home, not knowing that home is not a place but a manner of existence.

In her suffering she weeps and repents of her ignorance, and her prayer is heard. The spark of the divine glows red within her, and grace is given. She is chosen for the task of redemption, not because of her error but because of the spark in her which desires to return to the Father. The work of redemption is long and hard, yet the soul prepares herself to perform it, according to the will of the Father whom she no longer remembers.

The first part of the soul's work is to turn inward. The place of interiority is the womb of the soul. When she was occupied with the attractions of the visible world, she became enchanted into obliviousness concerning her past and her future. Turning inward, she begins to regain her proper character. She recognizes the charms of the visible world as illusions that enticed her from her true nature. By the will of the Father, the soul is baptized and cleansed of the pollution that was pressed upon her.

That some form of baptism or immersion in pure water was practised by the Jews as a ritual cleansing and a restoration to eternal life, goes back as far as Exodus (4:19-21), where Moses is commanded by the Lord to make a laver of brass and fill it with water, so that "Aaron and his sons shall wash with water that they die not." By the time the Jews (with John the Baptist) were baptizing, it was done with living water. Just as there is more mystery and fascination with a creek or river than with a bucket of water, so there was some similarity seen between the quickening of the water as it flowed over the rocks of a river, hastening the quickening of the spirit through repentance.

For us, whether we are men or women, repentance cannot occur unless we turn inward and seek self-knowledge. As long as we are fully outer-directed, we are unconscious of our own motivations. Driven by our fears, by loneliness, greed, willfulness and desperation, we see only the objects of our desires and not the mechanisms behind our efforts to satisfy them. Before the soul can emerge from her state of degradation, thoughts born of ignorance or willfulness and the actions resulting from them must be removed through something like ritual washing, until she is no longer contaminated. Only then will renewal be possible.

WAITING FOR THE BRIDEGROOM

The soul will begin to rage at herself like a woman in labor,
  who writhes and rages in the hour of delivery.
But being female, she is powerless to beget a child by herself.
The Father sends her man to her, her brother, the firstborn;
  the bridegroom comes down to the bride.
She has given up her former ways and cleansed herself;
  she is renewed so as to be a bride.
She adorns herself in the bridal chamber;
  she fills it with perfume.
She sits in waiting for the true bridegroom.

No longer does she run about the marketplace,
  copulating with whomever she desires.
She continues to wait for him, saying, "When will he come?"
She fears him, for she does not know what he looks like.
She no longer remembers, since she fell from her Father's house.
But by the will of the Father, she dreams of him
  like a woman in love with a man.

"The Exegesis on the Soul," *NHL*, p. 195

THE DESIRE FOR RENEWAL IS NOT easily fulfilled. Once the soul has recognized her faithlessness and repented, she feels her anger and self-hatred with full force because of what she has done to herself. She wishes to be worthy of the grace that has been bestowed upon her, but she is terrified that she will be found lacking and that no amount of cleansing and purifying will remove the stains of her transgression. Like a woman in labor, the hour of delivery comes whether she is pre-pared for it or not, and she cannot complete the process alone.

He descends to meet her, he who is that other aspect of her wholeness which has been forsaken by her, the one who is her brother, the firstborn, the archetypal Man. We have known him as the First Adam, or as Anthropos; Hindus call him Atman and Christians refer to him as the Christ. Indeed, the firstborn son of the alien and unknown God has been known by many names in diverse cultures. In human experience he appears in the psyche as the counterpart of the soul, and in this context Jung has called him "the symbol of the Self." In the gnostic narra-tive, he appears as the true bridegroom with the soul as his bride.

The soul as bride is cleansed and renewed. She is restored to her virginity, and all that she has suffered is like a horrific dream that vanishes in the light of dawn. She prepares the bridal chamber for herself and her bridegroom, making herself as lovely as possible. Who does not know the excitement of anticipating the lover who is the first true love of one's life? The soul waits with such an impatient patience, longing for him yet wishing for the tortuous rapture of her desire to be prolonged. She waits in delicious fear, savoring her curiosity about the unknown mate who will fulfil her and make her complete. She knew him once, when she was in the realm of the Father, but she no longer remembers him. And so she dreams, as we all dream, of the lost paradise or the lost innocence or the time that never was.

How splendid are the dreams of one who in is love with the glory of God!

THE SACRED MARRIAGE

The bridegroom, according to the Father's will,
    came down to her, into the bridal chamber
    which was prepared.
He decorated the bridal chamber.
And since that marriage is not like the carnal marriage,
    those who are to have intercourse with one another
    will be satisfied with that intercourse.
As if it were a burden, they leave behind them physical desire,
    and they turn their faces from each other.
But once they unite with one another, they become a single life.
Wherefore the prophet said of the first man and first woman:
    "They will become a single flesh."
For they were originally joined to one another
    when they were with the Father
    before the woman led astray the man, who is her brother.
This marriage brings them back together again
    and the soul is joined to her true love,
    her real master.

"The Exegesis on the Soul," *NHL*, p. 195

THE RITUAL OF THE SACRED MARRIAGE speaks to the archetypal union of heart to heart that surpasses every individual act. Entering the bridal chamber means taking a step into the hidden place where all that belongs to the rational world is laid aside. Here the opposites may be joined together in the most tender of relationships. Here boundaries are dissolved or broken through, and those who were unknown to one another become known in the fullest sense. Every part of their beings commingle with every part of the other until all separateness vanishes.

Marriage, the universal image of sexual union, also symbolizes in many cultures the union of opposites that are other than sexual. Sacred Marriage in mystery cults may represent the union of the human being with the god. It may also represent the union of a community with its celestial deity. For many, it is a sacrament in which the holy place is entered and where, through a communal meal, the substance of the One enters into the substance of the many. Among Jews at Passover the breaking of unleavened bread and eating it along with the wine and other elements of the symbolic wedding feast recalls the promise of the god of the Hebrews to be with his people always and to lead them back to their own country which they had abandoned in a time of famine, to go to Egypt. Jesus, commemorating the Jewish rite of his own people, broke bread and poured wine and shared these with his disciples in consummation of the relationship between the people and the One who came from beyond the stars.

The Sacred Marriage described in the gnostic text is not celebrated in remembrance of an event in the past, nor is it even a re-enactment of it. It does not come to pass because of knowing about the union of woman with man, or the union of person with divinity. The gnostic rite is actually taking place within the consciousness of the person who participates—at the very moment of partaking. All barriers dissolve as the wafers dissolve in the mouths of the bridal pair.

Because this is done according to the will of the Father, the Spirit is contained in the act. All that pertains to the physical world is left outside this bridal chamber, including all carnal desire. The statement "those who are to have intercourse with one another will be satisfied with that intercourse" strikes deeply into the sensibility of the soul, for she has known the carnal marriage and every perversion of it and was not satisfied, but now she will be satisfied. She will no longer strive to separate herself from an other, but will unite with him as her lover and they will become one. The two who were unbegotten, yet who emanated from the Father–Mother, had been lost to each other for many aeons during which the soul wandered over the lower worlds and came to know the ultimate in pain and suffering. Now the soul and the Self are rejoined as sister and brother and they become one, a single flesh.

RECOGNIZING THE BELOVED

Gradually the soul recognizes her beloved
   and she rejoices once more,
   yet weeping before him
   as she remembers the disgrace of her former widowhood.
She adorns herself still more,
   so that he might be pleased to stay with her.
He requires her to turn her face from her people
   and the multitude of her adulterers
   in whose midst she once was,
To devote herself only to her king, her real lord,
   and to forget the house of the earthly father
   where things went so badly with her,
But to remember her Father who is in heaven.
And the prophet said in the Psalms:
   "Hear, my daughter, and see, and incline your ear,
   Forget your people and your father's house,
   for the king has desired your beauty; he is your lord."[19]

"The Exegesis on the Soul," *NHL*, p. 196

IN THE VERY MOMENT WHEN THE SOUL is joined to her beloved, she weeps before him. Why, we wonder, was she allowed to fall or to descend into the world of form? When she was with the Father they were one and she was at peace. But she separated herself by a thought, and the primal unity was broken. Why is it necessary that the soul undergo shame and humiliation over and over again at the hands of the powers of this world? Why must she be deceived and seduced, raped and ravished?

We might as well ask why the innocence of an infant is not permitted to endure throughout her entire life. The first separation of the child from its mother is a necessary catastrophe for the child. She does not know whether the mother who has walked away will ever return. She begins to perceive the world with her own eyes, no longer trusting in the same way that the mother will always take care of her. This is the painful beginning of consciousness. Gradually, as she develops, she grows farther away from her parents and begins to make her own way in the world. She will stumble and fall many times. She will meet with trials and temptations; often she will err, and she will come upon difficult times. She will experience pain and loss, grief and desire, and she will become entangled in sensual experience, as represented by the archons. She will remember vaguely that there was a place of joy and peace. Memory traces surface from time to time, casting doubt upon what she does in the world. Dreams torment her; she finds no rest.

She does not know that her suffering comes about through the will of the Father. He subjects her to ordeal after ordeal, not out of anger because she has acted without his agreement, but out of his wish to recover the sparks of his glory that have been lost in the world, and to return them to the Light. The archons, too, desire to take possession of the sparks and thereby to raise themselves to the level of human beings in whom they are concealed. The Father sends his messenger to enter into the struggle for the liberation of the sparks. This furious struggle takes place in the human soul where the archons do their work, and there the hapless soul must strive to protect the holy spark.

How much suffering must we endure before we can begin to know our true selves? The allegory suggests that life requires of us that we submit to many kinds of experiences so that we may comprehend what we are made of. In order to gauge our strength we must be tempered by fire. It is an easy thing to praise the gods when they shower us with blessings. But when we have lost everything, our virtue, our pride, even our sense of who we are, it is not so easy to cry out for help to an alien God. The unknown God, like the absent mother, is far away from us and we are not even sure that he exists. Yet the very act of calling out to God leads us toward an awakening of consciousness.

THE WAY OF ASCENT

When the soul had again adorned herself in her beauty,
    she enjoyed her beloved and he also loved her.
And when she had intercourse with him,
    she got seed from him that is the life-giving spirit,
    so that by him she bears good children, and rears them.
For this is the great perfect marvel of birth,
    and this marriage is made perfect by the will of the Father.
Now it is fitting that the soul regenerate herself
    and become again as she formerly was.
The soul then moves of her own accord.
She receives the divine nature from the Father
    for her rejuvenation so that she might be restored.
This is the resurrection from the dead;
    the ransom from captivity.
This is the way of ascent to the Father.

"The Exegesis on the Soul," *NHL*, p. 196

THE CONSUMMATION OF THE SACRED marriage of the soul and the Self is not an ending, but a beginning on another level of consciousness. As the soul had once conveyed the breath that brought life to carnal man, Adam, so now does the Self bring eternal life through intercourse with the soul. The seeds of the Spirit are placed in her womb so that she may bring forth beings in whom the Spirit of the Father lives. This is the perfect marriage, the one that must come to pass within the individual before it can transpire between one person and another or between ourselves and the mystery of the All.

To be whole means to be at one with the divine Self. Wholeness is the original condition of life, before the first thought enters and begins to discriminate "this" from "that." Although we were whole at the moment of our birth, our lives become more and more fragmented as we live in the world. Each moment demands something else from us and we are pulled away from our center. We lose our sense of the natural rhythms of life and of the Light that empowers their harmonious actions. We become like automatons, going where we are led by the information that is fed to us, by the fashions of the times, and by the words of those whose wisdom we fail to question. We become as the living dead. This used to be called "loss of soul," but in our time it is termed depression, ennui, or complacency.

When the soul emerges at last from this darkness and is able to see with new eyes, we are free to move of our own accord. We can discriminate between those who are deceiving us and those who are worthy of our love. We are no longer captives in the web of senses and emotions, but can move as the Spirit moves in us, with perfect freedom. This is the meaning of "resurrection." It happens in the here and now, when consciousness is enlightened. The upward journey, the ascent into heaven, is a practice in which we engage—not an end that we must seek. Renewal is not "being born again." It is an ongoing process that, like a garden, requires continuous hard work to bring forth an abundance of excellent flowers and fruit.

MEDITATIONS AT SUNSET

According to what thou, great Life,
saidst unto me, would that a voice
might come daily to me to awaken me,
that I may not stumble. If thou callest
unto me, the evil worlds will not entrap
me and I shall not fall prey to the Aeons.

from "The Great Book of the Mandaeans"

ƑIRST THOUGHTS—VESPERS

IN THE TRADITION INHERITED FROM Judaism, monastic communities reckoned the hours of the day from sunset to sunset. Feast days began with the setting of the sun. Vespers is an hour of special importance because it comes at the end of the day's worldly tasks. It is a domestic prayer to be said at the time of coming home to the place of interiority, the abode of the spirit. Vespers is also called *lucernarium* because candles are lighted at this service. As darkness comes upon the world of measured time, Vespers reminds us to kindle the light within us, that it may dispel the twin shadows of inattention and ignorance. When the day's work is finished and time is taken for the inner life, the spirit is free to roam at will—to reflect, to contemplate and to give expression to itself.

"The Hymn of the Pearl,"[20] a charming poetic narrative, has been chosen for this hour because it deals with the threshold realm between the mundane world and the eternal world. Its hero is a prince, the divine child of divine parents, who is sent forth on a quest in which he will lose himself in order to find himself. The texts from which this tale is taken are not included in *The Nag Hammadi Library*. They are probably pre-Gnostic and pre-Christian. Its present form suggests a Manichaean origin, with the prince possibly representing Mani himself. This selection differs from all the others we have read in *Knowledge of the Heart* in that it appears in the first person as a narrative of one individual's experience. Although "Thunder: Perfect Mind" was also phrased in first person language, the very paradoxical nature of its pronouncements indicates that the speaker was not addressing her audience from a personal perspective but from that of a transcendent feminine being. Because the prince of "The Hymn of the Pearl" reveals his experience in simple and moving terms, we can easily identify with him.

The poem begins with the prince as a child living in a state of comfort and opulence with his celestial family, presided over by the divine Mother–Father. As long as he is engulfed in the archetype of wholeness, the prince is unaware of the visible world and his role in it. Like any child in a well-ordered household, his needs are taken care of without his having to be concerned about them. He is not destined to remain indefinitely in a state of childish innocence, however. One day his parents send him off into the world and give him a seemingly impossible task to perform. He is sent on a particular mission but, being naïve, he has no idea that the real purpose of this mission is to allow him to be instructed concerning how to achieve a level of consciousness suitable for an heir to the Kingdom. Leaving the matrix of the primordial psyche, he sets forth into the world on a great adventure in the course of which he will undergo trial and temptation. He will not return in the same condition as when he departed.

This sojourner's tale, told from the point of view of the masculine ego, has a very different quality from "The Exegesis on the Soul" with its description of the descent and subsequent ascent of the feminine soul. While both ego and soul seek to be reunited with the transpersonal Self—the soul, being reflective, is painfully aware of her separation and alienation, while at the

beginning of "The Hymn of the Pearl," the prince, as ego, is bliss-
fully unaware of the purpose of his journey. Whereas the soul's
task was to contemplate and reflect on the meaning of her life,
the ego's task is to awaken to the discovery of his own identity.

The might and majesty of this tale is transmitted to us as
through the mouth of one who speaks from a mystical state. All
that transpires here is a vision that may only be seen when the
veils of ordinary reality become transparent. Then the so-called
reality of the visible world is seen in dull sepia tones, while the
world of mystery shines and shimmers in a myriad of iridescent
shades and hues.

THE PRINCE DEPARTS

When I was a little child living in the palace of my father,
  in the luxury and wealth of those who nurtured me,
  my parents sent me away,
  out of the East, our native country.
They put together a bundle of treasures for me,
  both great and light, that I might carry it alone.
Gold and silver, and rubies from India they gave me,
  opals and pearls from the land of Kushan,
  and they girded me with adamant, which can crush iron.
They removed from me the garment set with gems
  and spangled with gold,
  which they had made for me, measured to my stature,
  because they loved me.
They made a covenant with me,
  and inscribed it in my heart so that I should not forget it.
"If you go down to Egypt and bring back from there the One Pearl
  which is there in the midst of the sea
  and is surrounded by the devouring serpent,
  you will put on again your robe of glory
  and will become, with your brother who is next to us,
  heir in our kingdom."

AGES BEFORE THIS STORY BEGINS, the Pearl of ines-
timable value has fallen out of the invisible world into the
dark sea of unconsciousness. It is a fragment of the holy Light,
but it gets mired in mud and slime and is encased in a common
shell. It can only be uncovered and retrieved down in the depths
where it has been swallowed up by the powers of the world,

symbolized as the devouring serpent who must be overcome from within. There the serpent crouches with his tail held in his mouth, encircling the original chaos. The precious treasures which the parents give to the prince to take on his journey are their transmundane spiritual instructions, the gnosis, which he is to communicate to those who have ears to hear.

The prince's true home is in the East, the place of the Fullness, the world of Light where the soul longs to dwell. His parents, the unknown Mother–Father God, send him off to "Egypt," which stands for the lower worlds. Upon his departure, they strip the prince of his marvelous robe of glory that shimmers like the stars. This fabulous garment has been fashioned to fit him exactly because his parents have taken his measure, that is, they know his limitations and his potential. With great love they send forth their divine son. They covenant with him that if he goes into the world of form and finds the One Pearl, and if he succeeds in wresting it from the grasp of the dark serpent power, he will be accepted back into the world of the Spirit.

The "prince" has many meanings for the gnostic, and also for us. In the invisible world he is the archetypal son of Man. When he descends from the "East," he becomes the spiritual essence that holds the power to enliven the souls who live in the visible world. As messenger from beyond the sphere of the rational, he is for us a bringer of light, a guide on the way, a doorway into another dimension of experience. He represents the person who comes into the world with a sense of purpose or mission, and who hears himself called to serve the One who summons him.

The brother who remains is the timeless twin we have met in other contexts. We may experience him in ourselves as that aspect which comes alive as we search out the divine Self within, the residue of the primordial spirit breathed into Adam and passed on to all the generations. We may visualize him as standing

guard over us, knowing what we are here for, watching whether we lose our way, and occasionally prompting us as to which way to turn. This "brother" does not get enmeshed in the visible world but waits to receive us in the invisible world.

IN AN ALIEN COUNTRY

I departed from the East by a difficult and fearful road
    with two royal guides, for I was very young to travel alone.
I crossed the borders of Maishan,
    the gathering place of merchants of the East,
    and reached the land of Babel and the walls of Sarbug.
But when at last I entered into Egypt my guides left me.

I set forth by the quickest way to the serpent,
    and by his hole I waited, watching for him to fall asleep,
    that I might take the Pearl from him.
While I was waiting all alone, a stranger in an alien land,
    I saw one of my own race, a free-born man from the East,
    a son of princes, or an anointed one.
I made him my companion and friend,
    I shared with him my mission and my journey.
I warned him to beware of the Egyptians
    and against consorting with the unclean.
Then I put on a robe like theirs, lest I appear
    as one who had come from afar to take away the Pearl
    and they arouse the serpent against me.

WHEN WE WERE VERY YOUNG we knew nothing of order or rule, but responded spontaneously to our instincts and feelings. If our parents were wise they did not interfere with our innocence or freedom, at least not until we began to have a sense of who we were and of the presence of others in our surroundings. We were guided and protected within the family for a reasonable period of time, but sooner or later we had to enter into the institutions of the wider society, leaving Paradise behind. We found ourselves in a place that seemed alien to us, an "Egypt." Gnostics used the name "Egypt" to stand for the world of matter, ignorance, and subservience to false gods. Those lacking gnosis were "Egyptians." In this land, this Egypt, the cult of the dead flourishes. Here we are asked to accept dead knowledge, assumptions that have been handed down generation by generation through traditions that leave no room for questions. No validity is given to the knowledge that arises of itself in the heart of the individual. Like the ancient people of Israel who were cast into bondage, we become inured to our plight and we take our pleasure from the food given us to sustain us and the drink given us to numb our senses.

The prince is still cognizant of his mission when he enters Egypt. He moves swiftly in the direction of the Pearl, the knowledge of his true self. He hurries to the edge of the sea and waits by the hole of the serpent for him to fall asleep. But the worldly one is not so easily overtaken. While the prince is waiting, he recognizes one of his own race, a person who has not succumbed to slavery—a fellow gnostic, one might say. So there are others in the world of form who have knowledge of the Light! One can trust such people, and can speak to them about a secret mission. The prince warns his fellow traveler, and thereby reminds himself of the dangers of becoming too involved with the Egyptians.

Nevertheless, propinquity works its effects. The prince, like any reasonable person, does not wish to appear conspicuous in enemy territory so he puts on a robe like those of the Egyptians to protect himself from the world's rulers. The impure garments allow him to gain access to the world of the Egyptians and to become familiar with it. But this ruse designed to outwit the archons defeats its purpose of safeguarding the prince, because it places him in the position where he is expected to partake of their meat and drink. Thus we are shown that compromising with the worldly powers is a two-edged sword, and the swordsman must be skilful indeed to avoid being beheaded with his own weapon.

THE SLEEP OF FORGETFULNESS

I know not how they discovered
    that I was not their countryman.
They dealt with me treacherously;
    they mixed me drink with their cunning
    and gave me to taste of their meat.

I forgot that I was a son of kings,
    and I served their king;
I forgot the Pearl for which my parents had sent me.
Because of the heaviness of their food
    I fell into a deep sleep.

LIKE THE PRINCE, WE OFTEN PUT ON the garments of our companions, adapting to the circumstances that surround us in the hope that this will make us more effective in what we wish to do, and that we will encounter less interference. Over our shoulders we drape this thin mantle, this "habit" that conceals our individuality. We believe that no one can see through it to discern that we are not wholeheartedly a part of the enterprise in which we pretend to be engaged. We delude ourselves into believing that however different we may be, we will be accepted as members of their society when, in reality, we are alien to it. As long as we are aware of the presence of the spirit in us and remain attuned to the subtle sound of its voice, we will appear different to others, even though those others may not be able to grasp exactly what is different about us.

    Some religious and spiritually oriented groups maintain their exclusiveness through dietary laws and practices which make it difficult, if not impossible, to break bread with members of other groups and thereby to enter into social intercourse with them. These laws have little to do with physical health or hygiene, much more with spiritual consistency. Those who hold to the tenets of their own society do not wish to be corrupted with the ideas of another group, a possibility that might increase as familiarity with the out-group grows. Eating together is inclusive; restricting the people with whom one will eat is exclusive. And so, through meat and drink, group autonomy is preserved and alliances are established.

When the prince eats the food of the Egyptians he is subverted into their state of numbness and sleepiness. He enters into the state of the "dead in the underworld," which is how the gnostics thought of the earthly existence. Infected by the poison of darkness, he falls into a deep sleep. Time passes slowly, and generations of humanity follow one another while the messenger from the East sleeps the sleep of oblivion in the land of his exile. He might have said:

> I dwelt in the world of darkness for thousands of myriads of years and nobody knew of me that I was there ... Year upon year and generation upon generation I was there, and they did not know about me that I dwelt in their world.[21]

If we are in a state of unconsciousness such as this, the soul slumbers in matter. It totally abandons itself to the visible world. We do not only sleep; we come to love the sleep. We no longer remember the beauty and the wonder of the treasure we once so eagerly sought.

THE CALL TO AWAKEN

While I slept the sleep of oblivion in Egypt
    my parents knew and grieved for me.
And it was proclaimed in our kingdom
    that all should meet at our gates.
All the kings and princes of Parthia
    and all the nobles of the East wove a plan on my behalf
    so that I might not be left in Egypt.
They wrote a letter to me
    and every noble signed it with his name.
"From your father, the King of Kings,
    and your mother, Mistress of the East,
    and your brother, who is next in rank,
    to you, our son, who is in Egypt: Peace!
Awake! Get up from your sleep!
Listen to the words of our letter!
Remember that you are a son of Kings,
    you, who have come under the yoke of slavery.
Remember the Pearl for which you went into Egypt!
Remember your robe of glory
    and the splendid mantle which you may wear
    when your name is read out in the book of the valiant,
    and when you and your brother inherit our kingdom."

THE UNKNOWN GOD BEYOND THE stars is Father-Mother to the wanderer in the visible world. The celestial pair know where their child is, even when he himself has forgotten his true home and no longer knows who sent him forth and for what purpose. The order of the universe remembers all its parts, whether in the invisible or the visible world. When ignorance, oblivion, forgetfulness and sleep prevail in the lower worlds, the disharmony is reflected in the realms above. The All sees it and seeks to restore its original unity. The drama of the eternal play of opposites is re-enacted scene by scene: the fullness of the light, the dynamic separation that occurs when the light is sent forth, the shattering of the vessels that should have received the light but were incapable of containing it, the fragmentation and dissemination of the sparks throughout the lower worlds and, finally, the shifting of direction toward ingathering or redemption.

The fate of the Pearl now parallels the destiny of the prince: both are hidden from sight, submerged in the filth and detritus of a decaying world, their splendid lustre obscured, their true identity forgotten. But in the larger plan, in the tapestry of infinity, neither prince nor Pearl is forgotten. The All longs for the ones who are lost. The Parents grieve. When they judge the time to be ripe they bring about an ingathering of the spirit in all its formless forms, "the kings and princes and nobles of the East." These weave a plan, the fabric of the order of the universe, by which they write a letter and each one signs his name to it. In this way they make themselves known to those who inhabit the visible world and who have ears to hear. They will send this message from their dimension to ours.

The letter itself is the Messenger who breaks into our lives to awaken us from our sleep and to remind us who we are, from where we have come, what is our true vocation and what is our ultimate destiny. Once more we will have an opportunity to become aware of the prince who lies dormant within us. We will be able to see into what a sorry plight he has fallen: how the worldly powers have made him their slave and then abandoned him.

The promise of the original covenant is renewed and set before us once more. We have been awakened, and our excitement is high. But this is not enough. The task for which we were sent to this place has not yet been accomplished. We must arise up from our slumber and take action.

CHARMING THE SERPENT

My letter had been sealed by the King with his right hand
 to keep it from the wicked ones, the children of Babel,
 and from the savage demons of Sarbug.
It flew in the form of an eagle, the king of birds;
 it flew and alighted beside me, and became speech.
At its voice and the sound of its rustling wings
 I started, and rose up from my sleep.
I took it and kissed it; I broke its seal and I read,
 and I realized that the words on the letter for me to read
 were the words written in my heart.

I remembered that I was a son of Kings,
 and my freedom longed for its own nature.
I remembered the Pearl for which I had been sent to Egypt.
I began to charm the terrible serpent;
By chanting the names of my parents over him
 I hushed him to sleep and lulled him into slumber.
I seized the Pearl,
 and turned to carry it back to my parents' house.

THE LETTER FLIES IN THE FORM OF an eagle, the great bird who soars higher than any other. It lives in the full light of the sun; it is luminous in its essence and it shares in the elements of air and fire. Its flight is swift and sure, swooping with lightning speed between the upper and the lower worlds. What more appropriate messenger to send from the East than the king of birds! Containing its magnificent power, the eagle must have settled down gently beside the prince, for at first all the prince hears is the rustle of feathers. He awakens as if from a deep dream; the eagle has become speech—yet somehow it is still the letter that has been sealed by the King with his right hand so that its contents are not accessible to those who are unable to rouse themselves from the sleep of oblivion which the archons have imposed.

The seal of the royal family is familiar to the prince although he has not seen it for a long time. He recognizes it and, because he is the son of the King, he does not hesitate to break it. He kisses the letter and opens it. This gentle act re-establishes the relationship between the prince and his parents, and between his sojourn in this world and his life in the world beyond. As he reads he comes to the realization that the words of the letter are the same as the words engraved in his heart but which, even so, he had forgotten.

Now he remembers who he is, a member of the royal family, a participant in the divine order, an offspring of the Most High. What has awakened him is the urge to liberate that which was submerged in him, as in all humanity, and that ever and again stirs people to throw off the manacles binding body, mind or soul. That urge is the spark that longs to be free, that it may rise to where it is truly "at home." This is the meaning of the Pearl which was forgotten, but is now remembered. But freedom, like the Pearl, is not given; it has to be dearly bought.

With the swiftness of the eagle, the prince hastens to the place of the serpent. The text says "I hushed him to sleep and lulled him into slumber." There is the hint of a magic charm here, the power of light over darkness. Darkness has the capacity to dim the light, but light obliterates darkness; so also does ignorance deface truth, but consciousness of our divine origin makes ignorance vanish. When the prince chants the sacred names of the Mother-Father over the serpent, the base element of the earth is depotentiated. In the name of the unknown Father–Mother, the son is able to redeem the Pearl.

FILTHY GARMENTS

I stripped off the filthy and impure garments
   and directed my way toward the light of our home, the East.
On my way, the letter which had awakened me
   was lying on the road.
As it had guided me with its voice,
   so now it guided me with its light.
It was written on Chinese silk,
   and shone before me in its own form.
Its voice soothed my fear and its love urged me on.

My robe of glory which I had taken off
   was sent to me by my parents
   in the hands of the treasurers,
   whom they trusted.
I had forgotten the robe's splendor
   for I had left it in my Father's house
   when I was a child.

THE PRINCE TURNS AWAY FROM the world of appearances and, discarding his impure garments, he directs his steps toward his true home. The letter that awakened the prince had preceded him, and now it is a letter of light written on Chinese silk, the most precious fabric of the East. Its light and its voice emanating from the divine Mother-Father guide him on his way. With every step he becomes more sure of the path and more secure in the knowledge of who he is. When he was a child living in the palace of his parents, he did not know where he was. Now that he has been away for a long time, during which he has forgotten much and remembered much, he knows in his heart the place of his origin. Then the wonder happens! The parents who have been watching over the prince through all his ordeals, send him his marvelous robe by their trusted emissaries. He had forgotten the beauty of the garment that had clothed him as befitted one of royal estate. Its splendor dazzles him. He is amazed to discover that he had left it behind and had given no further thought to it.

Casting aside the garment of the Egyptians means that if we would undergo a transformation of consciousness we will need to examine the modes of adaptation we have acquired over the years and determine whether or not these are appropriate to the person we are becoming. Most of us found it necessary from childhood on to make certain concessions to others which masked our true nature. Not wanting to be out of step, not wanting to be perceived as strange, or as a stranger, we disguised ourselves in order to resemble everyone around us. We did this, or so we told ourselves, in order to be accepted or esteemed or paid or loved. The mask became an instrument for dealing with the situations in which we found ourselves, and in time we hardly noticed that what we were wearing was not a part of us.

All this might have been necessary in the past in order to achieve a certain stability and self confidence. But, as consciousness increases, we come to understand that these adaptations are mere mechanisms, to be discarded when no longer needed. When our sense of values shifts from personal survival issues to the call of the spirit within us, we no longer need to carry around all that we formerly thought was necessary. We wish to become lighter. Useless possessions, relics of a time we have outgrown, ideas no longer relevant, all these can be dropped off as we begin the journey to our true home. Relieved, we walk with a more buoyant step. Unburdened, we experience a new freedom.

Only then are we ready to receive once again the robe that we left behind, along with our innocence, as we became absorbed in the chaos of the visible world. What has been carelessly put away need not be lost forever, but may reappear when we have come to know its value.

THE ROBE OF GLORY

All of a sudden as I faced it,
    the garment seemed to me like a mirror of my self.
I saw in it all my whole self, but divided in two,
    and yet one, in one likeness.
The treasurers also who brought me the robe
    I saw in like manner; they were twain, yet one likeness.
They restored to me the bright embroidered robe
    colored with gold and beryls and rubies and opals.
All its seams were fastened with adamant
    and the image of the King of Kings was embroidered upon it.
I saw it quiver all over with the movements of gnosis.
As it moved toward me I heard the sound of its tones saying:
    "I am the one who acted for him
    for whom I was reared in my father's house
    I saw myself growing in stature, according to his labors."
With the beauty of its colors I adorned myself
    and ascended to the Gate of Salutation and Adoration.
I bowed my head before the majesty of the Father who had sent it.
I had fulfilled his commandments
    and he had fulfilled what he promised.

THE ROBE OF GLORY THAT HAS BECOME the figure of the "true self" acts like a mirror. It reflects the prince in his twinship, his doubleness. When he now looks upon the treasurers who brought the robe to him he sees that they also are whole, yet divided in two. We are led to understand that this is the condition of human beings and gods alike; the temporal reality and the timeless reality are "the two in one." The robe represents the original or archetypal idea of both person and godhead: in each, the one aspect is preserved in the upper realms while the other labors down below.

The robe is a living entity that grows in size with the deeds of the one to whom it belongs, and is perfected by his travail. Its jeweled beauty and the permanence implied in its seams fastened with adamant, hard as a diamond, make it a suitable reward for the fulfillment of the task that life sets forth for the wayfarer. It also signifies his release from exile in the visible world.

The marvelous robe quivers with the movements of gnosis, revealing that it has remained in the house of the Father–Mother all the while the prince was fulfilling his task in the visible world. As the prince acted, the robe reflected his actions; as the prince grew in stature, which here means consciousness, the robe grew to fit him. The robe is the same as the brother whom the prince left behind. The hidden spark in the terrestrial being is reunited with its heavenly original who has been waiting for him all the while. Together they will inherit and rule the Kingdom.

The celestial parents rejoice in the return of the prince and they receive him in the company of the nobles. They promise to accompany him speedily on the journey to the Gate of the King of Kings. With his gifts and his Pearl, the prince will appear before the King of Kings.

Before us is the very center of the gnostic vision: our task is to discover the transcendent inner principle that has been called the Self, fragments of which reside in the human soul. Our supreme concern is to be about its care and its destiny. For those with eyes to see and ears to hear, it is a living presence both within and without. The inner spark desires to be reunited with the holy light of the Spirit—the King of Kings—beside whom there is no other. Thus the Pearl is returned to the One from whom it came forth, even as our own lives return to the flowing stream of Life itself.

NIGHT MEDITATIONS

The prophet saith:
"Seven times a day have I given praise to thee."

Psalm 111:164

"Commune with your own heart upon your bed, and be still."

Psalm 4:4

ℱIRST THOUGHTS
— COMPLINE

COMPLINE IS THE LAST OF THE SEVEN Day Offices. This meditation time comes after supper, upon retiring to bed. Inasmuch as the Offices are determined by the length of the day according to the daylight hours, Compline is said when darkness has settled in. Each person withdraws from the concerns of the day and retreats into the solitary inner space that no one else may enter. After Compline no word may be spoken until rising in the middle of the night for the Night Office. The call to prayer comes out of the silence itself, "Return, ye children of men."

The end of the day can also be a time for us to re-enter the maternal space of the unconscious. We no longer need to think, only to reflect. Events of the day may pass before us, but they do not matter now. They belong to another time, another place. Compline is a time to let go of the visible world, to let the mind and body rest, and to turn to the interior being who dwells within us. In the fading consciousness she is close to us and we are allowed to caress her gently. Soon even she drifts out of sight, and there is nothing left but silence and darkness and blessed repose. And then, there is nothing.

WORLDLY NAMES DECEIVE

Names given to the worldly are deceptive;
    they divert our thoughts from what is correct
    to what is incorrect.
Thus one who hears the word "god"
    does not perceive what is correct,
    but perceives what is incorrect.
So is it also with "the father" and "the son"
    and the "holy spirit" and "life" and "light"
    and "resurrection" and "the church" and all the rest.
People do not perceive what is correct
    but they perceive what is incorrect
    unless they have come to know [gnosis] what is correct.
The names which are heard in this world deceive.
If they were in the eternal realm,
    they would at no time be used as names in the world.
Nor were they set among worldly things.
They have their meaning in the eternal realm.

"The Gospel of Philip," *NHL*, p. 142

I**N DARKNESS AND SILENCE WE SHIFT** our attention from one reality to another. What seemed to be clear enough in the light of day becomes less certain after night has fallen. Words no longer hold the meaning for us that they once did. At night it is possible to recognize that words are nothing but arbitrary signs that the authorities have agreed upon in order to formulate ideas or to describe objects. Words bestow limitations on our perceptions. What are words anyway, but sounds emitted from the throat or squiggles of ink upon a sheet of paper, or letters of light on a cathode ray tube? That words are necessary to carry on complex communications no one would argue, but words are always "about" something; they are not the thing itself. They give a thing a name, but the name is not the thing. Yet the thing becomes identified with the name, and soon we find ourselves believing that the thing is what it is called and that it responds in the way people say it responds and acts as people say it acts. A subtle fabric of deception is built up. The more sophisticated the means of communication, the more effective the deception. It diverts us from our own observations and captivates us with the manifold descriptions by which it disguises reality.

When darkness and silence come upon us, we have no need of words or concepts or deceptions of any kind. It then becomes possible to see with the inner eye, which pierces the veils that separate the worlds. At such times we can observe that individuals give their own personal meaning to the words they utter. We all hear the names given by others in the context of our own frames of reference. Whenever we believe that when we hear a name, we know the person, we are incorrect. How much more, then, are we incorrect when we blindly accept the proclamations of those in authority who presume to describe such mysteries as "god" and "the father" and "the son" and "the holy spirit," which they have not seen and do not know!

It is in the dark of the night when the earth's face is turned away from the source of light, that the inner light may awaken in us. Then we may truly see—not from the midst of the deceptions that surround us—but as though from the eternal realm. If we have come to know what is correct, that is, if we have gnosis, it becomes clear to us that the names which we hear in the visible world are not the true names. The names that are used in the eternal world are not used in the temporal world, for they would have no meaning in the language of that world. To have meaning in the eternal realm requires a way of knowing that is not dependent upon the conventions of a particular place or society. Wordless contemplation and reflection, when there is no light save the light within, leads the seeker toward the perception of what is correct.

THE VIRTUE OF SILENCE

One single name is not uttered in the world,
> the name which the Father whispered to the son;
> it is the name above all things,
> the name of the Father.
For the son would not become the Father
> unless he wore the name of the Father.
Those who have the name know it, but they do not speak it.
But those who do not have it do not know it.

"The Gospel of Philip," *NHL*, pp. 142–3

B EYOND ALL THAT IS UNKNOWN is a single great mystery. This mystery is the name of the one whom we call "God." God is not the true name of the unknowable One, but only our word for what we do not understand. In our ignorance, we create our own gods and give names to them. It is written in the gnostic "Gospel of Philip": "God created man; ... men create God. That is the way it is in the world—men make gods and worship their own creations. It would be fitting for the gods to worship men!" Thus the gnostic declares his disdain for the gods and goddesses of men, all fashioned in the images of those who made them, or in the images of whatever was precious to their makers. Because of this, the gods of worldly passions and worldly possessions should be counted as lower than the sons and daughters of the primal couple. It would be fitting for the gods to worship humans because a breath of the divine wind (*pneuma*) was breathed into Adam and the light of the Epinoia was in Eve; hence we, their offspring, are more than the gods who created us and the ones whom we, in turn, have created.

But even so, what can any of us know, and which of us can encompass with the mind, the magnitude of that which exceeds the boundaries of our imagination? Only the highest God alone, the one we call "God," or "Father," knows who he is. No one who is less than that One will hear his true name uttered in the world. If we think of the Father as light, then the son is like a candle lit by the fire of the Father; if we think of the Father as wind, then the son is like the inbreath and the outbreath. The Father, through the medium of the son, transmits the light, the breath and whatever else signifies the Spirit, to all humanity. Not everyone recognizes or accepts these gifts. The "name" is whispered by the Father to the messenger, who hears, and who takes the light and the breath and puts it on as a garment. When he is truly seen by those who have eyes to see, he will appear as the Father, that is, as light or as breath.

This may be why many Jews do not await a Messiah who will come down in physical form, but hold instead an expectation of a Messianic Age when all who live on earth will wear the garment of holiness, and when the holy name will be enacted by those who have put on that garment through the way they conduct their lives. Nor will there be any need to speak the name as the authorities proclaim it. For to name something is to define it, and also by implication to say what it is not. Nor will there even be a possibility of speaking it, for the mantle of the divine Self, the robe worn by the princely son of the King of Kings, is of a splendor that defies description. Whoever puts it on will shine with the glory of gnosis. Those whose eyes are open will see it, while those who ignore it will see nothing.

THE HIDDEN AND THE REVEALED

Jesus took them all by stealth.
He did not appear as he was,
> but in the manner in which they would be able to see him.
He appeared to them all.
He appeared to the great as great,
> and to the small as small.
He appeared to the angels as an angel,
> and to men as a man.
Because of this, his word hid itself from everyone.
Some indeed saw him, thinking they were seeing themselves,
> but when he appeared in glory on the mount he was not small.
He became great, but he made the disciples great,
> that they might be able to see him in his greatness.

"The Gospel of Philip," *NHL*, pp. 144–5

THE HIDDEN IS HIDDEN FOR A VERY good reason. If a diamond were lying in the dust of the road amid pebbles crushed by the wheels of passing carts, it is unlikely that we would see it. We are more likely to see things in places where they are expected to be. It is said in "The Gospel of Philip," "No one will hide a large valuable object in something large, but many a time one has tossed countless thousands into a thing worth a penny. Compare the soul; it is a precious thing and came to be in a contemptible body." For this reason the wise speak in parables: of wheat and corn to the farmer, of dollars and cents to the merchant, of children and bread to the house-holder. The hidden is revealed through the evocation of what is already known; the inner knowledge of each individual is touched and thereby brought to life.

Gnosis links the great and the small in a paradox. It suggests that the awesome mystery, the unity of all things in a world beyond the capacity of human beings to imagine, can certainly be communicated to ordinary people. The mystery appears to all of us, to each in ways that we can understand according to our own particular mode of perception. It shows itself in the course of our daily pursuits, for it is hidden in every aspect of the mundane world. When we do not recognize the source of our ideas and insights, we tend to believe that they are our own but, in fact, they are formed in us by all the forces that act upon us and within us. Ideas flood in on us from every direction, from the world of matter with its emphasis on facts and material things and from the world of psyche with all its concepts and rationalizations. Gnosis is present in us also, but it abstains from public display. Unless we are constantly attentive to what lies beneath the obvious, unless we persistently remove the layers of surface noise while we plumb the depths for the sound of the whispering voice, the source of wisdom goes unnoticed and people ascribe their cleverness and ingenuity to themselves alone.

We are told that in the darkness there is no difference between the person who is blind and the one who is able to see. But when the light comes, then the blind one remains in darkness and the other is bathed in the light. We cannot see more than what our eyes are able to behold, but when the fire of the spirit is made manifest all things are possible, as it is said: "It is through fire and water that the whole place is purified—the visible by the visible, the hidden by the hidden. There are some things hidden through those visible. There is water in water, there is fire in chrism." ("The Gospel of Phillip," *NHL*, p. 144)

THE OPPOSITES WITHIN

I

Light and darkness, left and right, are brothers of one another;
    they are inseparable.
Because of this, neither are the good good, nor the evil evil,
    nor is life life, nor death death.
Therefore each will dissolve into that from which it first came,
    the Undivided.
But those who are exalted above this world
    are indissoluble, eternal.

"The Gospel of Philip," *NHL*, p. 142

II

When you make the two one,
    and when you make the inside like the outside
    and the outside like the inside,
    and the above like the below,
    and when you make the male and the female one and the same
    ... then will you enter the kingdom.

"The Gospel of Thomas," (22), *NHL*, p. 129

I

THE FIRST TEXT PROCLAIMS THE intrinsic androgyny of the invisible world and explains the relationship of the opposites within the whole. The second refers to the visible world and its condition, and informs us what we must do in order to overcome the split in our own souls that alienates the spirit from matter and separates what we are from what we might become.

Light and darkness at first glance appear to be opposites and indeed, from the way the gnostics read these words, they apply to separate worlds and world-views; light being associated with all that is sublime and evanescent, and darkness with what is gross and impermeable. Light stands for Spirit, darkness for body, earth and matter in general. Let us consider our own experience of light and darkness: when we awaken in the dark from a deep sleep, or when we walk from the sunlight into a darkened theatre, at first we see nothing. But in a short while our eyes become accustomed to the darkness and gradually the soft edges of objects appear, and little by little we find that it is not completely dark after all. Our eyes have the marvelous capacity to adapt to the subtle existence of light within darkness. There is no time when darkness is not, and there is no time when light is not.

Likewise, matter and Spirit exist together in the world of form, always and ever, and their existence is also a part of the experience of the human soul. As dark and light are relative one to the other, so also with good and evil, and life and death. In this world of form, we tend to see these as separate and distinct, at least until we reflect upon their nature; but in the eternal world, we can see that the opposites dance together in a close embrace, that they love one another and wish to remain together.

II

Here in the visible world that we inhabit for a limited number of years, we are charged with beginning to unite the opposites within ourselves. This is our way of preparing ourselves for the moment when we will depart from this life and dissolve into something other. Then all separations will become meaningless. If we realize this while we are still in these bodies, then we will know that to discriminate between man and woman, or race and race, or rich and poor, is to allow ourselves to be trapped in an illusion that will prevent us from entering "the kingdom," which we here understand as the place of integrity, that is, wholeness, within ourselves.

SEEING AND BECOMING

It is not possible for anyone to see anything of the things
    that actually exist unless he becomes like them.
This is not the way with the man in the world:
    he sees the sun without being a sun;
    and he sees the heaven and the earth and all other things,
    but he is not these things.
This is quite in keeping with the truth.
But you saw something of *that* place and you became *those* things.
You saw the spirit, you became spirit.
You saw Christ, you became Christ.
You saw the father, you shall become father.
So in *this world* you see everything and do not see yourself.
But in *that world* you do see yourself—
    and what you see you shall become.

"The Gospel of Philip," *NHL*, pp. 146–7

GNOSTIC TEXTS ARE TYPICALLY structured both to conceal the message from those who through ignorance might misuse it and to reveal the meaning to those initiates who are committed to the world of light. To the gnostic, a statement may mean exactly the opposite of what it appears to mean. The gnostic is given to understand that the secret meaning of this seeming distinction is that it is apparent but not real. We are reminded of the well-known dichotomy between *this world* and *that world*. Both worlds exist within us and they are not separate. To the degree that we are aware of this, we are gnostic in our perception; while those who see *this world* and *that world* as "real" and "unreal," or as "here" and "hereafter," are in error, according to the gnostic view. Then what are the entities we call *this world* and *that world*, if not reality? They are concepts, those tricks of the mind we play when we try to explain the inexplicable. Through these tricks, the mystery becomes a thing and the thing gets submerged. The Pearl is buried in the slime, guarded by the serpent who would keep the treasure for his own, for it inevitably seems to those in power that they must maintain their power by controlling whatever is of value to others.

In *this world*, the visible world, we see ourselves as separate from the objects around us. We do not identify ourselves with the forces of nature or with the divine—these all are outside of us and act upon us; or if we are sufficiently powerful, we act on them. We do not see our own role in our relationship with the created world, or with the invisible world. This is natural in a world that is viewed as fragmented. But from the standpoint of *that world*, we are not separate, for we have thrown off the garments that previously distinguished us one from another. Reflecting upon *that world*, we recognize ourselves in whatever we see with the inner eye, the eye that beholds the vision of unity. The two worlds dissolve in us and we dissolve in the fullness of the One.

RESURRECTION BEFORE DEATH

I

You who say you will die first and then rise are in error.
If you do not first receive the resurrection while you live,
    when you die you will receive nothing.

"The Gospel of Philip," NHL, p. 153

II

They are wrong who say, a heavenly man exists and one above him.
For the first of these heavenly men, the revealed one,
    they call "the one who is below;"
    and the hidden one is supposed to be above him.
It would be better for them to say, "the inner and the outer,"
    and "what is outside of the outer."
Because of this the lord called the outer darkness "destruction,"
    and there is nothing outside of it.

"The Gospel of Philip," NHL, p. 150

III

He said, "My Father who is in secret."
Therefore go into your chamber, and shut the door behind you,
    pray to your Father who is in secret,
    the One who is within them all.
Beyond it is nothing else.

"The Gospel of Philip," NHL, p. 150

I

WHEN WE RETIRE FOR THE NIGHT it is well to remember that every sleep is a "little death," and every morning a "little resurrection." Unless we live in awareness of the cycle of death and rebirth throughout our lives, we relinquish our chance for resurrection because resurrection occurs now, in this world, rather than hereafter, in that world. A Messenger breaks into our daily routine to startle us with a challenge. We are to create in this world the likeness of what we envisage the other world to be!

II

The Redeemer might make us think of "two heavenly men:" the Second Adam who came to earth in the form of an image of the First Adam who was formless, and who is subordinate to the one "above him." The gnostic understands that this is incorrect. The two refer to dual aspects of the Redeemer figure, one which exists outside of us and the other, the indwelling savior.

The human mind, with its bent for categorization, may well ask, What is outside the outer? It is a question that betrays our difficulty in living with ambiguity. This is tantamount to saying that mystery always cries out for solution. But of the ultimate Mystery there can be no solution. So once more, we are forced to deal with the conundrum: What can there be that would exist outside the Totality, outside the All? Surely, no thing. However this answer is not likely to be satisfactory, because our logical minds cannot help imagining the All as something, as opposed to no thing, or nothing. Therefore, the lord ingeniously provides a better answer, he calls the outer darkness "destruction." Whatever we imagine the outer darkness to hold, destruction immediately destroys it. If the darkness were truly outside the world of light, it could not exist; it would vanish as the night vanishes in the daylight.

III

These insights relieve the turning and tossing mind of its burden, and release it from its toils. In silence and in solitude, without the burden of the critical intellect, we are able to address the Father who is in secret. To go into your chamber and shut the door behind you is to enter the Holy of Holies, the interior sanctuary where only one can enter. It is like the desert of the solitary one, the place where the hidden may be revealed.

FIRE AND WATER

I

I have cast fire upon the world, and see,
I am guarding it until it blazes.

"The Gospel of Thomas," (10), *NHL*, p. 127

II

Glass decanters and earthenware jugs
    are both made by means of fire.
But if glass decanters break, they are done over,
    for they came into being through a breath.
If earthenware jugs break, however, they are destroyed,
    for they came into being without a breath.

"The Gospel of Philip," *NHL*, p. 147

III

Those who have gone astray, whom the spirit itself begets,
    usually go astray because of the spirit.
Thus by one and the same breath,
    the fire blazes and is put out.

"The Gospel of Philip," *NHL*, p. 146

IV

Through water and fire the whole place is purified:
the visible by the visible, the hidden by the hidden.
There are some things hidden through those visible:
there is water in water, there is fire in chrism.

"The Gospel of Philip," *NHL*, p. 144

I

THE INCOMPREHENSIBLE ONE SPEAKS in fire. He is lord of the powers that have neither form nor substance: lightning, thunder, wind and fire. The ancient gnostics looked upon these elements as signs that the Spirit is possessed of energy that cannot be grasped or contained by human hands. By the will of God, they say, sparks from the divine light fell upon the created world and found refuge in the hidden recesses of the human heart. The heat shocks us into awareness of their light in us, the light of gnosis. Unlike the gods of the Greeks who tried to keep the fire from humanity, the Eternal One sends a Messenger to stand guard over us until the spark begins to glow as inner wisdom.

II

Two kinds of individuals are likened to the earthenware jug and the glass decanter. The first is solid and opaque, being made of earth. When shattered it is destroyed, because there is no life in it. The glass decanter is delicate and transparent. Formed by the breath blown into it, glass can be melted down in fire and formed again through the breath. Likewise, when we become conscious of the Spirit within us, we do not lose our lives when our bodies are broken but we are re-shaped and transmuted into other forms.

III

Spirit, like fire, can become too intense for those who do not know how to approach it. Silence and solitude can shield us, say the gnostics. Those who have no ears to hear are inclined to shout, "Look, look, see that I am enlightened!" and they are burned up in their own fireworks. Spirit is the breath of life; its presence sustains us when we respond to its call with willingness to serve it, but it destroys us when we use it only for our own ends.

IV

Fire and water purify matter; but it is not ordinary water and fire that purify the soul. It is the Water that is hidden in the water, and the Fire that is hidden in chrism, that purify the soul and prepare it to receive the spirit. The Water in the water is the Maternal Presence: the sea from which all life springs, matrix and womb, tomb and burial ground. She cleanses the soul of its ignorance. The Fire is the presence of the Father in the consecrated oil, the source of light. These we may receive when we enter into the presence of the mystery.

Know then, before the curtain
of night obscures knowledge,
that the truth is to be sought in
this world and also in *that world*,
for the two worlds in truth are
one; it is only the rational mind
that thinks otherwise.

Notes

1   *Corpus Hermeticum IV*, 8, cited in Jonas, *The Gnostic Religion*, p. 52.

2   Psalm 137:1.

3   Or archetypes, we would say.

4   The third son of Adam and Eve, who was endowed with knowledge from the Tree of Knowledge.

5   V. Tcherikover, *Hellenistic Civilization and the Jews*.

6   Page references throughout refer to The *Nag Hammadi Library* (*NHL*) (J. Robinson, ed.), Harper & Row, San Francisco, 1998.

7   The monad is described as a spiritual being that is one and indivisible, unchanging, indestructible, impenetrable, and unknowable, a center from which all the physical properties of matter, all thought, and all inspiration are derived.

8   When referring to gods, we, of course, include goddesses as well.

9   By the time that the "Apocryphon of John" was written, the term "archon" had become entirely pejorative. Since the world was created by the demiurge, the archons ruled over a realm in which both spirits and humans were in themselves evil.

10 Greek word meaning "plenitude" or "fullness."

11 Epinoia is a Greek word meaning "insight."

12 Ironically, the Gnostic version of this biblical tale rationalizes the behavior of the serpent.

13 Adam's name comes from the Hebrew *adamah*, meaning earth.

14 Reprinted with the gracious permission of Bishop Rosamonde Miller of the Gnostic Center, Palo Alto, California.

15 The numbering of the texts from "The Gospel of Thomas" follows that used in *The Nag Hammadi Library*.

16 *Didymus* in Greek and *Thomas* in Aramaic both carry the meaning of "twinship."

17 Literally "the word," the *Logos* often refers to the "living Jesus" or the Redeemer figure.

18 Jewish followers of Jesus and his teachings.

19 Psalm 45:10–11.

20 The hymn exists in an early Syriac text and in a somewhat later Greek text that was inserted into the apocryphal Acts of Thomas. "The Hymn of the Pearl" as it appears here in the readings for Vespers is the result of combining and interweaving portions of three separate versions of the hymn; from Willis Barnstone's *The Other Bible*, pp. 308–13; Robert M. Grant's *Gnosticism*, pp. 116–22; and Montague Rhode James's *The Apocryphal New Testament*, pp. 411–15.

21 From "The Great Book of Mandaeans," cited in Hans Jonas, *The Gnostic Religion*, p. 54.

SUGGESTED READING

For those who wish to pursue their explorations into the sources of the mystical traditions in Judaism and Christianity, the following volumes are recommended:

The Nag Hammadi Library, James M. Robinson (ed.), 1988. The complete translation of the Nag Hammadi Library into English by the Claremont team of scholars, with appropriate introductions to the entire volume and to each book within it. A basic source book.

The Gnostic Scriptures: Ancient Wisdom for a New Age, Bentley Layton, 1987. A new translation of many writings generally considered to be Gnostic, including some of the Nag Hammadi books as well as important texts from other sources. Written by a noted scholar, with annotations and an introduction, these ancient scriptures reveal much that was hitherto unknown about the historical roots of Gnosticism in Christian theology and classical Judaism.

Gnosis, Kurt Rudolph, 1983. Probably the best and most comprehensive introduction to ancient Gnosticism available in English (and other languages) at this time. Rudolph surveys the sources for our knowledge of the Gnostic religion and discusses in rich detail the essential ideas of the Gnostic movement as well as its various cultic, social and ethical structures. It is enhanced by illustrations, including some color photographs of Manichaean artwork.

The Gnostic Religion, Hans Jonas, 1963. A valuable summary of the basic philosophical ideas and themes of Gnostic literature. It discusses the main tenets and how they are expressed through the symbolic language used by the Gnostics. The Gnostic movement is placed within the cultural context of Hellenism.

The Secret Books of the Egyptian Gnostics, Jean Doresse, 1986. Exceptionally interesting is the author's description of his role in the discovery of the Nag Hammadi texts. Also included are some of the earliest translations of certain texts, along with his critical comments.

The Gnostic Gospels, Elaine Pagels, 1979. The Gnostic texts are related to the social reality of the times when they were written. A fascinating account of the struggles between the Gnostics and the priestly authorities of the day. This lively book is written by a scholar for the general reader.

Gnosticism and the New Testament, Pheme Perkins, 1993. A survey of the origins of Gnosticism, its relationship to Judaism, Redeemer myths, New Testament hymns and other relevant topics.

The Gnostics, Jacques Lacarrière, 1977. An extended meditation on the lives, beliefs and practices of the ancient Christian heretics, written with elegance and outrage.

The Allure of Gnosticism: The Gnostic Experience in Jungian Psychology and Contemporary Culture, Robert A. Segal, Murray Stein and June Singer (eds.), 1995. A collection of 16 essays that range from near classic treatments by well-known scholars such as Gilles Quispel, Hans Jonas, and Edward Conze, to new approaches by writers of very diverse orientations including historians of religion, Jungian analysts and, in one case, a gnostic bishop speaking from her own experience.

The Other Bible, Willis Barnstone (ed.), 1984. A collection of ancient esoteric Jewish, Christian, and Gnostic texts that were not included in the Bible, along with excellent introductions to each section. Included are creation myths, histories and narratives, Wisdom literature and poetry, Apocryphal Gospels and Acts, apocalyptic literature, diverse Gnostic texts and mystical documents including material from the Dead Sea Scrolls, the Zohar (Kabbalah) and the mystical theology of Pseudo-Dionysius (Christian). A useful glossary of mystical terms is appended.

BIBLIOGRAPHY

Apocrypha (E. J. Goodspeed, trans.), University of Chicago Press, Chicago, 1938

Barnstone, W., (ed.) *The Other Bible*, Harper & Row, New York, 1984

The Holy Bible (Revised Standard Version), Thomas Nelson & Sons, New York, 1952

The Book of J (translated by David Rosenberg and interpreted by Harold Bloom), Grove Weidenfeld, New York, 1990

Borges, J. L., "The lottery in Babylon," in *Labyrinths*, New Directions, New York, 1964

Doresse, J., *The Secret Books of the Egyptian Gnostics*, Viking Press, New York, 1960

Friedman, R. E., *Who Wrote the Bible?*, Summit Books, New York, 1987

Grant, R., *Gnosticism*, Harper & Brothers, New York, 1961

Hennecke, E. and Schneemelcher, W. (eds.), *New Testament Apocrypha*, vol. 2, Westminster Press, Philadelphia, 1965

Hoeller, S., *The Gnostic Jung and the Seven Sermons to the Dead*, The Theosophical Publishing House, Wheaton, Illinois, 1982

Johnson, P., *A History of the Jews*, Harper & Row, New York, 1987

Jonas, H., *The Gnostic Religion*, Beacon Press, Boston, 1963

Jung, C. G., *Aion, Collected Works 9, ii*, Princeton University Press, Princeton, 1951/1968

Jung, C. G., *Psychology and Religion: West and East, Collected Works 11*, Princeton University Press, Princeton, 1958/1969

Jung, C. G., *Mysterium Coniunctionis, Collected Works 14*, Princeton University Press, Princeton, 1955–6/1970

Jung, C. G., *Memories, Dreams, Reflections*, Pantheon Press, New York, 1973

King, K. (ed.), *Images of the Feminine in Gnosticism*, Fortress Press, Philadelphia, 1988

Lacarrière, J., *The Gnostics*, E.P. Dutton, London, 1977

Layton, B., *The Gnostic Scriptures,: Ancient Wisdon for a New Age*, Doubleday, New York, 1987

MacDonald, D. R., *There is No Male and Female*, Harvard Dissertations in Religion, Fortress Press, Philadelphia, 1987

Pagels, E., *The Gnostic Paul*, Fortress Press, Philadelphia, 1975

Pagels, E., *The Gnostic Gospels*, Random House, New York, 1979

Pagels, E., *Adam, Eve, and the Serpent*, Random House, New York, 1988

Perkins, P., *The Gnostic Dialogue: The Early Church and the Crisis of Gnosticism*, Paulist Press, New York, 1980

Parenti, S., *Praying with the Orthodox Tradition*, (P. Clifford, trans), Triangle, London, 1989

Quispel, G., "Gnostic Man: The Doctrine of Basilides," in *The Mystic Vision: Papers from the Eranos Yearbooks*, Bollingen Series XXX. Vol. 6, Princeton University Press, Princeton, 1968

Quispel, G., *Studies in Gnosticism and Hellenistic Religions*, E. J. Brill, Leiden, 1981

Quispel, G. "Gnosticism from its Origins to the Middle Ages," in *The Encyclopedia of Religion*, M. Eliade (ed.), Macmillan, New York, 1987

Robinson, J. (ed.) *The Nag Hammadi Library*, Harper & Row, San Francisco, 1988

Rudolph, K., *Gnosis*, Harper & Row, New York, 1983

The Rule of St Benedict (J. McCann, trans.), Sheed and Ward, London, 1989

The Rule of the Master (L. Eberele, trans., monk of Mount Angel Abbey), Cistercian Publications, Kalamazoo, Michigan, 1977

Segal, A., Stein, M. and Singer, J. (eds.), *The Allure of Gnosticism: The Gnostic Experience in Jungian Psychology and Contemporary Culture*, Open Court Publishing, Chicago, 1995

Scholem, G., *Jewish Gnosticism, Merkabah Mysticism and Talmudic Tradition*, Jewish Theological Seminary of America, New York, 1960

Tcherikover, V., *Hellenistic Civilization and the Jews*, The Jewish Publication Society, Philadelphia, 1959